INDIAN ENGLISH

A Bibliographical Guide to Resources

INDIAN ENGLISH
A Bibliographical Guide to Resources

L.S. RAMAIAH

GIAN PUBLISHING HOUSE
DELHI-110007

GIAN PUBLISHING HOUSE
29/6, Shakti Nagar, Delhi-110007
Phone : 7213053

ISBN 81—212—0236—1

PRINTED IN INDIA

Published by Mrs. Gayatri Garg for Gian Publishing House, Delhi and Printed at Godwall Printers, Delhi.

Dedicated to

Professor C.D. Narasimhaiah
with profound admiration
for his work at Dhvanyaloka, Mysore

PREFACE

LANGUAGE change is a historical fact and the development of language varieties—regional, national, social and other —is inevitable. But the direction which these changes take is determined by various conscious and unconscious attitudes of the users of the language in question apart from the new setting in which it comes to be used. India has been one of the biggest and the most variegated settings in which English has come to stay, and in the past few years the attitudes of its users have not only converged but stabilized. The English language has received the status of a second language as distinct from that of a foreign language. As such it now serves the communicative needs of a signficant (if not large) section of the Indian population.

It is the attitude of the users, again, that determines the purpose or purposes for which they ultimately employ the language. In our own sub-continent the English language has come to serve a variety of important functions—the instrumental the regulative, the interpersonal and even the imaginative. The, functions for which a language is used determines in its turn the nature of changes that take place. Thus the peculiar Indian setting—geographical, social and cultural—the distinct attitude of its people to the English language and the purposes for which the language has been employed, all these have contributed to the 'Indianization' of English. And the existence of a broad variety of English which can be called 'Indian English' has tacitly been recognized.

However, the choice of a variety as a model for teaching and learning English in India has bcen a moot point. There are still people who *feel* that British Englsh should be the model, at least as far as the written form is concerned. This choice is a Hobson's choice because conscious prescription in any pedagogical context should follow description. Descriptions of British English are ample and often so inviting that we have sometimes tended to substitute mere description for the knowledge of the language itself. And if there is some scepticism about choosing Indian English as a model for teaching and learning, it is probably because comprehensive descriptions of Indian English are not yet available. When they become available, it will not only be possible to correlate sub-varieties of Indian English with their functions, but make a conscious choice of a variety for pedagogical purposes. It may well be an educated sub-variety of Indian English.

Talking of sub-varieties does not make sense sometimes because these often cut across one another. While educated and non-educated varieties are distinguishable in terms of certain features which may be largely common to the distinction in British as well as Indian varieties, there would be certain features which are peculiar to the registral varieties of either. For example, I believe that within the educated Indian variety, writings on science and technology are likely to be not too different from their British counterparts, while those on philosophy, religion or fine arts are likely to be significantly different. Scientific and technical writings are likely to be least Indian in character as compared to writings on philosophy, religion and fine arts which are likely to display a good deal of Indianisms. These will have to be studied carefully before a choice of model is consciously made.

On the other hand, the use of English for the purposes of imaginative writing, particularly fiction, has received some attention. Descriptions of what is often called experimentation with language in Indian writing in English has on the whole received a stamp of approval, and even appreciation. This has not only contributed to the body of critical writings on literature in English but largely vindicated the stand of many an experimenter. But then instances of experimentation with language are not necessarily features of Indian English. And yet some of them may well be. And so there is a long way to go even in this area of study.

Obviously, all this calls for coordinated and concerted research efforts on the part of linguists, ELT experts and literary critics towards producing descriptions of Indian English. There is no gainsaying that bibliographies are a starting point for any research enterprise, and this Indian English bibliography should be welcomed for more than one reason. This is the first most comprehensive bibliography of works on Indian English both synchronically and diachronically ; it lists works dating from 1788 to date, almost two centuries in breadth, and what is more, the entries are classified into ten well defined sections. In the case of general works further referencing for Indian English is also provided.

This preface will be incomplete without a word about its compiler Mr. L.S. Ramaiah. He is one of the very few librariasu in India who have taken the reference librarian's role very seriously. He has proved to be a source of unfailing guidance to researchers in the field of English studies being pursued at the Central Institute of English and Foreign Languages. He has compiled a number of bibliographies on specific areas of ongoing research, some of which have been published and some mimeographed. This Indian English bibliography is a timely addition which I am sure will give a further spurt to research on different aspects of Indian English.

Kolhapur

S.V. SHASTRI

INTRODUCTION

ENGLISH is today a window on to the world. Approximately 700 million people around the world speak English. It is the mother tongue of 300 million people in 12 countries and in 33 countries 300 million people use it as a second language while in 56 countries 100 million people use it as a foreign language. English is the foremost foreign language studied in schools in many different countries and according to one estimate, seventy-six per cent of secondary school children in the non-English speaking world excluding China, are now studying it.

Furthermore, English is the international language of aviation, the most common medium for international broadcasting and it is estimated that it is used for seventy per cent of inter-national mail. As such English is now everyone's second language, and has a life of its own in totally non-English situations. A Japanese businessman might learn it to strike trade deals in Brazil. A Russian might learn it to do research in Berlin. An Indian might learn it to practice some profession or the other in Canada, U.S.A and England. In Salman Rushdie's words 'English, no longer an *English* language, now grows from many roots ; and those whom it once colonized are carving out large territories within the language for themselves'.

English came to India with the English traders in the 17th century. With the gradual expansion of the rule of the East India Company over India, English became the language of communication between the rulers and the ruled. As a result of the famous minute of Thomas Macaulay in March 1835, English was introduced in the Indian schools. The aim of Macaulay's Minute was simple : 'to form a class who may be interpreters between us and the millions whom we govern ; a class of persons, Indian in blood and colour, but English in taste, in opinions, in morals, and in intellect'. This was the turning point which established English firmly on the soil of the Indian sub-continent.

English had till 1947 been playing the role of the common language between the British rulers and their Indian subjects. It was the official language of the Raj. It was dethroned from this position only after the Indian independence in 1947. However, English is still recognised as an 'associate' official language. Professor Lal, a champion of English in India, claims that in simple numerical terms 'more Indians speak English and write English than in England itself'. It is used at all levels of society. It is used in local English newspapers and broadcasting, in public administration, in university education, in the major industries, the courts and the civil service. English has come to stay in India along with the other constitutionally recognised official languages. It is the official language of Nagaland which is one of the constituent states of the Indian Republic.

The cross cultural spread of English round the world resulted in the creation of varieties of Englishes. Some of them are known as *Japlish*, *Swinglish*, *Spanglish*, *Hiberno-English*, *Indian English*, *African English*, *Bajan* (Barbadian English), *Yinglish* (Yiddish-English), and *Singlish* (Singapore English). Indian English is one such variety. It is neither a dialect nor a Pidgin but only a corrupt variety. There are infinite gradation of Indian English ranging from the less-educated varieties like Babu English, Butler English, Kitchen English to educated or standard Indian English, often very scholarly and bookish. Yule and Burnell in their famous book *Hobson-Jobson* described Indian English as follows :

> The broken English spoken by native servants in the Madras Presidency; which is not very much better than the Pidgeon-English of China. It is a singular dialect ... thus *I telling*=

'I will tell' ; *I done tell*='I have told' ; *done come*='actually arrived' ... The oddest characteristic about this jargon is (or was) that masters used it in speaking to their servants as well as servants to masters.

English and the Indian languages have influenced each other. Many of the distinctively Indian features of Indian English are common to most or all of the Indo-Aryan languages and several also found in Dravidian languages. In the area of phonology the features of Indian languages detailed below are instrumental to our Indian accent in English. They are :

1. Tenser articulation of Indian languages than English, with vowels produced further forward, leading to the loss of some distinctions between different vowels.
2. The pronunciation of the voiceless consonants /p/, /t/, /k/ without aspiration in all positions.
3. The pronunciation of the English alveolar consonants /t/ and /d/ as the heavier retroflex consonants /t/, /d/.

As in the case of phonology even in the other areas like vocabulary and grammar, the influence of Indian languages is evident in Indian English. All the Indian languages have borrowed extensively from English, especially in areas connected with modern institutions and technology. A compilation of such English loan words in all Indian languages has not yet been attempted. A Dictionary of English loans in Indian languages will help scholars to find out the impact of English in modernization of Indian languages. Dictionaries of Indian loans in English have already been compiled and published. In this connection the works of Yule and Burnell, Subba Rao, Ray Tongue, Nihalani and Priya Hosali, and R.W. Hawkins deserve commendation.

English, besides its tremendous uitility in education and administration, has been adopted by writers to the Indian experience. Indo Anglian literature is the oldest of the 'new literatures' in English. Cavelly Venkata Boviah (1776-1803) of Ellore in A.P. was the first great master of English prose. His contribution, a lengthy dissertation on Jains, appeared in the Asiatic

Society's Journal in 1801. His work preceded the first English publication of Raja Rammohan Roy 'The Precepts of Jesus' (1820) by 19 years.

Indian writing in English which started as a trickle in 1801 grew tremendously in the present century. It has produced such outstanding writers as Sri Aurobindo, Mahatma Gandhi, Sarojini Naidu, Jawaharlal Nehru, R.K. Narayan, Raja Rao, Mulk Raj Anand, Nirad Chaudhuri and a host of others. The Indian English press contributed vastly in both pre- and post-Independence periods. Sixty per cent of Indian publicatications are still in English.

The Indian English discourse has become a subject of study for its linguistic, syntactic and stylistic features by scholars in Indian universities and abroad. A modest Indian English corpus has been collected by Dr. M.P. Jain of the Indian Institute of Technology, New Delhi, for studying the unique character of Indian English on computer. Prof. S.V. Shastri of Shivaji University has also collected a corpus of structures of Indian English Grammar for further study and analysis. These two databases will be of immense help to scholars working in the field of Indian English.

No systematic and exhaustive bibliography was available on Indian English. The absence of such a tool made the study and research in the area a time consuming and arduous task to scholars. Prof. Braj B. Kachru, University of Illinois, who contributed copiously on Indian English through his books and numerous articles, has suggested to the present compiler during one of his visits to the Central Institute of English and Foreign Languages, Hyderabad (India), the need for such a bibliography. The author is extremely grateful to Prof. Kachru for his suggestion. All sources available in India have peen consulted in compiling this bibliography and to make it as exhaustive as possible. The entries in this bibliography cover up to the end of 1987.

Hyderabad

L. S. Ramaiah

ACKNOWLEDGEMENTS

BIBLIOGRAPHIC control in humanities is not effectively organised in India. There is a need to set up a National Documentation Centre for Humanities. Scholars and researchers in these disciplines still grope in the dark and mostly rely on their own efforts for collecting information. Hence, the compilation of bibliographies in this area helps greatly both research scholars and librarians. In compiling this as well as my earlier bibliographies, I received help and inspiration from many outstanding teachers and others at the Central Institute of English and Foreign Languages, Hyderabad, India.

I am very much grateful to Prof. S.K. Verma, Director, CIEFL and Dr. K. Jayashankar, Registrar, CIEFL, for their constant encouragement and support in building up the library resources and preparation of bibliographical tools. They are a tower of strength for all academic activity at the CIEFL. I am also thankful to Prof. Ramesh Mohan, former Director, CIEFL and at present Vice-Chancellor, Meerut University, Prof. R.N. Ghosh, Prof. K. Subrahmanian, Prof. K.C. Nambiar, Prof. N. Krishnaswamy, Prof. B.V.L. Narayanarow, Prof. S.V. Pradhan, Prof. K.S. Yadurajan, Prof. K.A. Jayaseelan, Prof. V.D. Singh and Dr. K.V. Tirumalesh for their interest and inspiration from time to time in the preparation of this bibliography.

I am grateful to Prof. S.V. Shastri, Head of the Department of English, Shivaji University, Kolhapur, for kindly acceding to my request for writing a valuable preface to this work. My thanks are due to Ms. Anjuli Gupta, research scholar, Freie

Universitat Berlin, West Germany, for supplying information on some of he entries in this bibliography. I am thankful to Sri T.V. Prafulla Chandra, Professional Assistant, CIEFL, who typed the manuscript for the Press. I also wish to express my gratefulness to my friends Prof. R.S. Sharma, Sri G. Shivaram and Sri G.G.K. Gokhale whose conversations on topics of artistic beauty and otherwise over cups of tea during lunch breaks invigorated me to take my toil with cheer and fortitude,

Finally, I must express my thanks to M/s. Gian Publishing House, Delhi and Shri B.P. Garg through whose efforts this bibliography has seen the light of the day.

Author

CONTENTS

1. BIBLIOGRAPHIES

1. AGGARWAL, Narinder K. 1981
English in South Asia : A Bibliographical Survey of Resources. Gurgaon, Indian Documentation Service.

2. CARLS, Uwe. 1979
"Select Bibliography of Indian English (Upto 1978)." *Zeitschrift fur Anglistik und Amerikanistik*. 27 : 4. pp. 327-340.

3. CENTRAL INSTITUTE OF ENGLISH AND FOREIGN LANGUAGES (Hyderabad). 1972
A Bibliography of Indian English. Hyderabad, CIEFL. (See Part II).

4. ————. 1986
List of Research Dissertations. Hyderabad, CIEFL Library. (Mimeographed)

5. DAKIN, Julian. 1963
A Survey, with Bibliographical Notes, of the Discussion of the Medium of Instruction in India Since 1947. Thesis

(Ph. D.)—University of Leeds. (Certain portions deal with Indian English).

6. FISIAK, Jacek.(ed). 1983
A Bibliography of Writings for the History of the English Language. Poznan, Univwersytet Im Adama Mickiewicza W Poznaniu.

7. GORLACH, Manfred. 1979
A Selective Bibliography of English as a World Language 1965-78. Heidelberg, Universitat Heidelberg. (Also in : *Arbeiten aus Anglistik und Amerikanistik.* 2 (1979), pp. 231-268).

8. "Indian English (A Select List of Books and Articles)". 1970
Vartavaha. 5. pp. 18-20.

9. JACKSON, Howard. 1981
Bibliography of Indic Languages : Descriptive and Contrastive Studies. 2nd ed. Birmingham, Department of English and Foreign Languages, City of Birmingham Polytechnic.

10. KACHRU, Braj B. 1964
A Selected Tentative Bibliography of Studies on Indian English. Urbana, III., Department of Linguistics, University of Illinois. (Typescript).

11. ————. 1978
Selected Bibliography on South Asian English, (This is given at the end of the article "English, in South Asia".) *IN* FISHMAN, Joshua A. (ed) : *Advances in the Study of Societal Multilingualism.* The Hague, Mouton. pp. 523-537.

12. ————. 1983
Bibliography, *IN* KACHRU, Braj B. : *The Indianization of English : The English Language in India.* Delhi, Oxford University Press. pp. 241-261.

13. KUSHWAHA, M.S. 1972
English Research in India. Lucknow, Swastika.

14. LIMAYE, M.S. 1986
"Further Reading : A Select and Relevant Bibliography," *Seminar*. 321. May. pp. 46-48. (Special Issue on Indian English).

15. VERMEER, Hans Josef. 1969
Das Indo-Englische. Situation und Linguistische Beleutung (*Mit Bibliographie*). Heidelberg, Julius Groos.

16. VIERECK, W. ; SCHNEIDER, E. and GORLACH, M. 1984
A Bibliography of Writings on Varieties of English, 1965-1983. Amsterdam, John Benjamins.

---

2. GENERALIA

---

17. ACHARYA, D.R. 1967
"The Importance of English in Free India." *The Journal of English Language Teaching*. 2 : 5. pp. 159-160.

18. ALAM, Qaiser Zoha. 1983
Issues Linguistic and Pedagogic. New Delhi, Sterling.

19. ALLEN, D.O. 1854
"The State and Prospect of the English Language in India." *Journal of the American Oriental Society*. 4. pp. 263-275.

20. ALOK, R. 1984
"Language and the Media : Seeing Through the Newspaper." *India International Centre Quarterly*. 11 : 2. pp. 187-199.

21. ALSDORF, L. 1937
"Die Entstchung der Neuindischen Sprachen." *ZDMG.* 91. N.F. 16. pp. 423-447.

22. ANAND, Mulk Raj. 1948
The King-Emperor's English ; or the Role of English Language in Free India. Bombay, Hind Kitabs.

23. ————. 1969
"A plea for English for Higher Education". (An Open Letter to the Union Minister for Education.), *IN Language and Society in India : Proceedings of a Seminar.* Simla, Indian Institute of Advanced Study, pp. 279-291. (Also in : *Quest.* April 1969. pp. 30-39.)

24. ————. 1972
"Pigeon-English : Some Notes on Indian English Writing." (Paper read at the Seminar on Australian and Indian Literature, New Delhi, 1970). *Journal of Karnataka University (Humanities).* 16. pp. 69-90.

25. ————. 1975
"The rhythms of Indian Life on Indian English", *IN* RADHAKRISHNAN, N. (ed) : *Research and Criticism.* Annamalainagar, Research Scholars Association, Annamalai University. pp. 59-61.

26. ————. 1982
"The Taste of the Pudding", *IN* NARASIMHAIAH, C.D.and SRINATH, C.S. (eds): *English Its Contemporary Role in India.* Mysore, Dhvanyaloka. pp. 100-111.

27. ANANTANARAYANA, H.S. 1969
"Indian Elements in English." *The Hindu.* 19 October.

28. "The Anglo-Indian Tongue." 1877
Blackwood's Edinburgh Magazine. 121. May. p. 541-551.

29. ANNIAH GOWDA, H.H. 1980
"Regional Standards of English With Particular Reference to India." Paper Presented at the ACLALS Conference, Fiji, January 3-8.

30. ANSARI, Iqbal A. 1978
Uses of English : *Varieties of English and Their Uses.* New Delhi, New Statesman. (See chapters 4 for Indian English.)

31. ANSTEY, F. 1898
Baboo Jabbarjee, B.A. London.

32. ANTHONY, Frank. 1972.
"English in India : A Historical Appraisal Since 1947." *Indian and Foreign Review.* 10 November.

33. ARDHANAREESWARAN, B. 1984
"What Motivates Teacher Trainees of English as a Second Language in South India." *IATEFL Newsletter,* 81. pp. 26-28.

34. ARYA, Ramesh Chandra. 1977
"A Survey of the Use of English in India : Some Theoretical Pre-Requisites." *CIEFL Newsletter.* 24. pp. 5-10.

35. ASRANI, V.A. 1964
What Shall We Do About English ?" Ahmedabad, Navajivan.

36. AZRA, Sultan. 1981
"Case For English." *M.P. Chronicle.* 27 April.

37. "Baboo English." 1882
The Times (London). 11 April. p. 8 and 14 April. p. 13.

38. "Babu English." 1881
Chamber's Journal. 58. 31 December. pp. 840-842.

39. BAILEY, Richard W. and ROBINSON, J.L. (eds). 1973.
Varieties of Present-Day English. New York, Macmillan.

40. BAILEY, Richard W. and GORLACH, Manfred. (eds). 1982
English as a World Language. 2 Vols. Ann Arbor, University of Michigan Press.

41. BAINS, Harcharan. 1982
"English—Misplaced Emphasis." *Tribune.* 6 January.

42. BANDUKWALA, J.S. 1976
"English No Longer a Foreign Language." *Statesman.* 8 October.

43. BASU, Babu Ram Chandra. 1876
"The English-Speaking Natives of Upper India." *Indian Evangelical Review.* April. pp. 470-483.

44. BASU, J.N. 1979
The Romance of Indian Journalism. Calcutta, Calcutta University Press.

45. BAYER, Jennifer Mani. 1979
"Anglo-Indians and Their Mother Tongue." *Indian Linguistics.* 40 : 2. pp. 78-84.

46. BELYAEVA, T.M. and POTOPOVA, Y.A. 1961
Anglilskii Yazyk Za Predelyami Anglii (The English Language Outside England). Leningrad.

47. BERRY, J. (ed). 1976
"Language and Education in the Third World." *International Journal of Sociology af Language.* 8.

48. BHATIA, L.S. 1980
"India's English Dilemma." *National Herald.* 1 December.

49. BHATIA, Sugam Chand. 1975
"The Choice of an Instructional Model in English Language Teaching in India." *IRAL.* 13. pp. 152-152.

50. BHATNAGAR, C.P. 1977
"To Kill or Not to Kill : The Role of English in India and the Factors Threatening to Throttle it." *Modern Review.* 141 : 4. April. pp. 209-218.

51. BRITISH COUNCIL. 1960-61
The English Language Abroad. London, The British Council. (Extracted from the British Council's Annual Report 1960-61.)

52. BROUGHTON, Geoffrey. 1986
"Standard Indian English." *The Hindu.* 9 November. p. 16. (Reported by Tiivandrum staff reporter of *The Hindu.*)

53. BURTON, J.G. 1957
"The Teaching of English as a Foreign Language." *Shiksha : The Journal of the Education Department, Uttar Pradesh.* April. pp. 56-60.

54. ————. 1961
"Some Modern Misconceptions About the English Language and About Language Teaching Current in India." *Bulletin of the Central Institute of English.* 1. pp. 16-20.

55. BUTTER, P. 1960
English in India : An Inaugural Address Delivered at the Queen's University. Belfast, The Queen's University.

56. ————. 1973
"Some Indian Periodicals." *A Review of English Literature.* 4 : 2. pp. 35-44.

57. CAPTAIN, R.M. 1949
The Place and Teaching of the English Language and English Literature in University Education in India. London, Institute of Education, University of London. (Unpublished report for associateship.)

58. CARIAPPA, K.M. 1973
"The English Language in India", *IN* SUNDARA REDDI, G. (ed) : *The Language Prob lem in India.* Delhi National. pp. 58-64.

59. CARLS, Uwe. 1982
"The Status of English in India." *Linguistiche Studien* (Berlin). pp. 80-87. (Akkademie des Wissenschaften des DDR.)

60. CHALAPATHI RAU, M. 1963
"The Indo-Anglians." *The Illustrated Weekly of India.* 84 : 21. p. 45.

61. CHANDA, S.M. 1983
"Who Murders English ?" *Frontier.* 14 May. p. 13.

62. CHATTERJEE, Kalyan Kumar. 1976
English Education in India : Issues and Opinions. New Delhi, Macmillan.

63. CHAUDHRI, Harish Chandra. 1985
"The Role of English in India : Present and Future", *IN* BISWAS, A.K. (ed) : *Profiles in Indian Languages.* Kanpur, Indian Languages Society, I.I.T. p. 225.

64. CHAUDHURI, Nirad C. 1976
"The English Language in India : Past, Present and Future," *IN* NIVEN, Alastair (ed) : *The Commonwealth Writer Overseas.* Bruxelles, Librarie Marcel Didier A.A. pp. 89-105.

65. CHAUDHURI, Sukanta. 1983
"Living With English." *Statesman.* 17 and 18 July.

66. CHAVARRIA-AGUILAR, O.L. 1966
"English and Hindi in India : Their Respective Roles." Paper presented at a Conference on Language Problems of the Developing Nations at Airlic House, Warrenton, Virginia, 1-3 November.

67. CHIBBER, V.N. 1980
"English Has Come to Stay." *National Herald*. 10 July.

68. ————. 1980
"English-Need to Abjure Emotion." *Patriot*. 5 June.

69. ————. 1984
"English Now More Than Ever." *Patriot*. 14 August.

70. CLARKE, H. 1890
"The English Language in India and the East." *The Asiatic Quarterly Review*. 10, pp. 149-162.

71. CONRAD, Andrew W. and FISHMAN, Joshua A. 1977
"English as a World Language : The Evidence" *IN* FISHMAN, Joshua A. *et.al.* : *The Spread of English*. Rowley, Mass., Newbury House. pp. 3-76.

72. D.R. 1977
"What is Wrong With Indian English." *Times of India*. 18 September.

73. DAKIN, Julian. 1968
"Language and Education in India", *IN* DAKIN, Julian ; TIFFIN, Brian and WIDDOWSON, H.W. : *Language in Education : The Problem in Commonwealth Africa and the Indo-Pakistan Sub-Continent*. London, Oxford University Press. pp. 1-62.

74. DAS, Bikram K. 1972-73
"English for a Developing Country : A Plea for Linguistic Relativism in Teaching." *CIEFL Bulletin*. 9. pp. 18-26.

75. DAS, Mahajiteswar. 1977
The Needs for English in Orissa : An Investigation Into the English Language Requirements and Related International Programmes at the Post-Secondary Level of Education. Thesis (Ph.D.) Central Institute of English and Foreign Languages, Hyderabad.

76. DASWANI, C.J. 1982
"English in India : The Brown Man's Burden." *Literary Criterion*. 17 : 2. pp. 93-99.

77. ————. 1982
"English in India—The Brown Man's Burden", *IN* NARASIMHAIAH, C.D. and SRINATH, C.N. (eds) : *English Its Contemporary Role in India*. Mysore, Chvanyaloka. pp. 93-99.

78. DASWANI, Tilottama. 1963
"The English Language and Its Contribution to Indian Languages." *The Indian P.E.N.* 29 : 11. pp. 317-319 and 29 : 12. pp. 345-349.

79. DATTARAY, Suna K. 1981
"Humdrum in Any Tongue : But English Long to Reign Over Us." *Statesman*. 13 March.

80. DEB, S.C. 1965
Presidential Address Delivered at the 16th Conference of the Indian Association for English Studies, Jadavpur. Allahabad, R.G. Press.

81. DERRETT, M.E. 1962
"Why Write in English ? India's Search for Self-Expression." *Times Literary Supplement*. 61. No. 3154. 10 Aug.

82. DESAI, Maganbhai P. 1964
The Problem of English. Ahmedabad, Navajivan.

83. DHARMA KUMAR. 1886
"108 Varieties." *Seminar*. 321. May. pp. 33-35. (Special issue on Indian English.)

84. D'SOUZA, Austin A. 1953
"The British Legacy in India." *The Indian Review*. 54. pp. 52-54.

85. ————. 1973
"Future of English in India." *Educational Quarterly*. 25 : 1. pp. 20-23.

86. DUFF, Alexander. 1837
New Era of the English Language and English Literature in India. Edinburgh, J. Johnstone.

87. DUSTOOR, Phiroze Edulji.
"Dominion Status in Language." *Allahabad University Magazine*. (Talk from the All India Radio, Lucknow.)

88. ————. 1950
The English Language in India Today. Agra, Agra University. (Agra University Extension Lectures. 1-11.)

89. ————. 1957
"The Future of English in India.", *Allahabad University Magazine*. 35. pp. 1-18.

90. ————. 1957
"Presidential Address Delivered at the 7th Session of the All India Teachers' Conference, Dharwar, December 1966." *Shiksha : The Journal of Education Department, Uttar Pradesh*. April. pp. 61-71. (This address specifically discusses Indian English.)

91. EARLE, D. 1976
"Indian English." *The Hindu*. 2 November. (Letter to the Editor in Madras edition.)

92. ELIAS, Mohamed. 1978
"Mark Twain on Indian English", *IN* MANUEL, M. and AYYAPPA PANIKER, K. (eds) : *English in India*. Madras, Macmillan. pp. 181-189.

93. "The English Language in India." 1966
Modern Review. 119 : 6. pp. 505-509.

94. FENNELL, C.A.M. 1892
Preface, *IN The Standard Dictionary of Anglicised Words and Phrases.* Cambridge, Cambridge University Press.

95. FRIEDRICH, P. 1962
"Language and Politics in India." *Daedalus : Proceedings of the American Academy of Art and Science.* 91 : 3. pp. 553-559.

96. GANDHI, K.L. 1979
"Movement Against English as Official Language", *IN* ANNAMALAI, E. (ed) : *Language Movements in India.* Mysore, CIIL. pp. 91-98.

97. GOFFIN, R.C. 1934
Some Notes on Indian English. SPETract 41, Oxford, Society for Pure English. pp. 20-32. (SPETract No. 41.)

98. GOKAK, Vinayak Krishna. 1960
English in India : A National Perspective. Hyderabad, Kanganath Press and Publishing. (Presidential address delivered at the All India English Teachers' Conference, December 1960.)

99. ————. 1961
"English in India." *Educational Forum.* 6 : 1. pp. 28-31.

100. ————. 1964
English in India : Its Present and Future. Bombay, Asia Publishing House.

101. GUPTA, Shyam Ratna. 1984
"Weeds in the Garden of English." *Hindustan Times Magazine.* Sunday. 16 September.

102. HANCOCK, I.F. (ed). 1979
Krio, Varieties of English Around the World. Heidelberg.

103. HARRIOT, J.A. 1932
The English in India : A Problem of Politics. Oxford, Oxford University Press.

104. HENNESSY, Josselyn. 1969
"British Education for Our Elite in India", *IN* WILLIAMS, Rupert. (ed) : *Governing Elites.* New York, Oxford University Press.

105. HILL, Leslie A. 1961
"English in the Commonwealth : 1—Teaching of English in India." *English Language Teaching.* 15 : 2. pp. 49-56.

106. HOME, D.C. 1981
"Over a Century of Usefulness to the Nation—English Amar Rahe." *Blitz.* 28 February.

107. HUNT, Cecil. 1931
Honoured Sir-From Babujee. London, P. Allen.

108. ————. 1935
Babujee Writes Home. London, P. Allen.

109. "Indian English." 1969
Indian Writing Today. 3 : 2. pp. 3-6. (Editorial.)

110. IQBAL, Ahmad Ansari. 1979
Uses of English, Varieties of English and Their Uses. New Delhi, New Statesman Publishing.

111. JHA, Aditya Nath. 1940
Address at Conference of English Professors, Playwrights and Critics, Lucknow. (Includes extensive references to Indian English.)

112. JHA, Akhileshwar. 1976
"English Why Not ? " *Statesmen.* 23 May.

113. ————. 1978
"Why Not Indianise English." *Hindustan Times.* 19 November.

114. ———. 1981
"Importance of English——Pursuit of Excellence." *Times of India.* 9 July.

115. JOHN, George. 1977
"Is 'Indish' the Answer?" *Youth Times.* 2 September. pp. 44-45.

116. JOHN, V. V. 1981
"English Medium Schools." *Indian Express.* 17 March.

117. ————. 1969
The Uses of English, *IN* JOHN, V.V. : *Education and Language Policy.* Bombay, Nachiketa. pp. 50-62.

118. JUGAL, Kishore Chand, 1981
"English Has a Role—Why Not ?" *Mainstream.* 19 : 41. 13 June. pp. 27-28.

119. KACHRU, Braj B. 1965
"Language and Learning : Comments on *Indian Writing in English*, by P.Lal." *Harvard Educational Review* 35 : 1. pp. 71-75.

120. ———. 1980
"The Non-Native Literatures as a Resource for Language Teaching." *RELC Jonrual.* 11 : 2. pp. 1-9.

121. KACHRU, Araj B. and QUIRK, Randolph. 1981
Introduction, *IN* SMITH, Larry E. (ed) : *English For Cross-Cultural Communication.* London, Macmillan. pp. xiii-xx.

122. KACHRU, Braj B. 1982
"Language Policy in South Asia." *Annual Review of Applied Linguistics.* 3. pp. 60-85.

123. ———. 1986
"Review of 'VIERECK, W. ; SCHNEIDER, Edgar W. and GORLACH, Manfred : *A Bibliography af Writings*

on Varieties of English 1965-1983." *English World-Wide.* 7 : 1. May. pp. 132-135.

124. KANUNGO, Gostha Behari. 1962
The Language Controversy in Indian Education : A Historical Study. Chicago.

125. KHUBCHANDANI, Lachman Mulchand 1977.
"Language Ideology and Language Development : An Appraisal of Indian Education Policy." *Linguistics.* 193. pp. 33-52.

126. KAUSHWANT SINGH. 1974
"English Zindabad Vs. Angrezi Hatao." *Illustrated Weekly of India.* 95 : 2, 13 January. pp. 8-10.

127. ———. 1983
"Indo-Anglian Misunderstanding." *Hindustan Times* 2 April. p. 9.

128. ———. 1986
"Indish." *Seminar.* 321. May. pp. 36-38

129. KODANDA RAO, P. 1975
"English Language in India." *Tribune.* 16 February.

130. KOHLI, Devendra. 1978
"Indian English." *Statesman.* 9 April

131. KOPPAL, Sebastian. 1983
English in Sub-Und Sudostasien, *In English-Formen Und Funktionen Einer Weltsprache.*pp. 117-143.

132. KRISHANASWAMI, N. 1971
"Indian English ?" *NIE Journal.* 6 : 2. pp. 6-10,

133. ——. 1985
"The Growth of 'Inglish' in India." *The Hindu.* 3 December. p. 19.

134. KRUSINA, A. 1970
"Anglictina V Indii." *Sbornik Linguistickyen Praci* (Prah). pp. 96-118. (English in India,)

135. KUMAR, Raj. 1970
Presidential Address at the All India English Teachers' Conference Held at Bhubaneshwar, December 1970. (Discusses about 'Indish'.)

136. LAHIRI, K.C. 1958
"English in India." *Journal of Education*. 6 : 1. pp. 43-49.

137. LANHAM, H. W. 1978
"An Outline History of the Languages of Southern Africa" *IN* LANHAM, H.W. and PRINSLOO, K. P. (eds) : *Language and Communication in South Africa : Current issues and Directions in Research and Inquiry.* Capetown, Oxford University Press. pp. 24-25 of section 4 : 3 deal with Indian English.

138. ——. 1985
"The Perception and Evaluation of Varieties of English in South African Society", *IN* GREENBAUM, Sidney. (ed) : *The English Language Today.* Oxford, Pergamon Press. pp. 242-251. (See pp. 244-245 for Indian English.)

139. LE PAGE, R.B. 1964
The National Language Question : Linguistic Problems of Newly Independent States. New York, Oxford University Press.

140. LESTER, Mark. 1978
"International English and Language Variation." *ELT Documents*. 102. pp. 6-14.

141. LOTT, B. 1974
"Some Notes on the History of English in India." *Bulletin, Central Institute of English and Foreign Languages.* 10. pp. 1-12.

142. LUTZE, Lothar. 1969
"English and Hindi", *IN Language and Society In India: Proceedings of a Seminar.* Simla, Indian Institute of Advanced Study. pp. 190-195.

143. McCRUM, Robert ; CRAN, William and MacNEIL, Robert, 1986
The Story of English. London, Faber & Faber and BBC Publications. (For Indian English, see pp, 39-40, 175, 308, 324, 326-335 and 340.)

144. MAHALINGAM, Annumathy. 1983
"O! This English Language." *Amity International* (India). April. pp. 1-2.

145. MANUEL, M. and AYYAPPA PANIKER, K. (eds). 1978
English in India : Essays Presented to Professor Samuel Mathi. Madras, Macmillan.

146. MARIOTT, (Sir) John A.R. 1932
The English in India (A Problem of Politics). Oxford, The Clarendan Press.

147. MARRYAT, Florence. 1868
Gup : Sketches of Anglo-Indian Life and Character. London, R. Bentley.

148. MATHAI, Isaac. (ed) 1960
India Demands the English Language. Bombay, Mathai's Publication.

149. MATHAI, Samuel. 1951
The position of English in India, *IN* PATRIDGE, E. and CLARK, J. W. (eds) : *British and American English Since 1900.* New York, Philosophical Library. pp. 96-101.

150. ——. 1957
"English in India." *Shiksha : The Journal of the Education Department, Uttar Pradesh.* 9 : 4. pp. 91-97.

151. ——. 1974
"English For Unity." *Illustrated Weekly of India.* 95 : 1. 13 January. pp. 12-13, 15.

152. ——. 1979
Preface, *IN* NIHALANI, Paroo *et. al.* (eds) : *Indian and British English : A Handbook of Usage and Pronunciation.* Delhi, Oxford University Press. pp. V-VIII.

153. MEHROTRA, Raja Ram. 1971
"English in an Indian Context." *Hindustan Times.* 7 February. (Weekly Review.)

154. ——. 1971
"Indian English." *Hindustan Times Weekly,* 2 May. (A reply to Dr. B.B. Kachru's comment which appeared in the *Hindustan Times,* 11 April 1971.)

155. ——. 1974
"Dimensions of a Language Policy--The Case of English" *IN* SABERWAL, Satish. (ed) : *Towards a Cultural Policy.* New Delhi, Vikas. pp. 112-125.

156. ——. 1977
"English in India : The Current Scene." *English Language Teaching Journal.* 31 : 2. pp. 163-170.

157. ——. 1980
"Long Live Indian English." *Times of India.* 21 September.

158. MOHAN, Peggy. 1981
"English and the Indian Elite." *Indian Express.* 9 April.

159. ——. 1984
"Two Faces of a Language Death." *India International Centre Quarterly.* 11 : 2. pp. 133-145.

160. ——. 1986
"Postponing to Save Time." *Seminar.* 321. May. pp. 14-17. (Special Issue on Indian English.)

161. MOHAN, Ramesh. 1974
Presidential Address, *IN* The Proceedings of the All Indian English Teachers' Conference, 28-30 December, Department of English, Punjabi University, Patiala.

162. ——. (ed). 1978
Indian Writing in English: Papers Read at the Seminar on Indian English Held at the Central Institute of English and Foreign Languages, Hyderabad, July 1972. Madras, Orient Longman.

163. MOOS, S. N. 1965
"The English Language." *Swarajyva.* 9 : 43. pp. 9-12.

164. MUKHERJEE, Hiren. 1972
"The English Language and India Today." *Indian and Foreign Review.* 9 : 19. pp. 9-11.

165. MUKHERJEE, Shankar. 1984
"Is There a Future for Indian English ?" *Patriot.* 19 August.

166. MULJI, Rosaleen 1986
"Some Thoughts." *Seminar.* 321. May. pp. 17-23. (Special Issue on Indian English).

167. MULLICK, K. S. 1980
"Pidgin English." *The Hindustan Times Weekly.* 21 September. p. 9.

168. MURTHY, S.N. 1978
The English Language in India. Mercara, Murthy.

169. MUTHIAH, S. 1977
"Is English India's Vanishing Language?" *Indian Review* (Madras). 73 : 7. pp. 39-42

170. NAGARAJAN, Sankalapuram. 1976-77
"The Decline of English in India : A Historical Perspective." *Journal of the School of Languages.* 4 : 2. pp. 21-30.

171. ——. 1977
"Some Historical Notes on the Decline of English." *Journal of Higher Education.* 2 : 3. pp. 341-349

172. ——. 1978
"Decline of English in India : Some Historical Notes", *IN* MANUEL, M. and AYYAPPA PANIKER, K. (eds) : *English and India.* Madras, Macmillan. pp. 161-171. (Also in : *College English.* 43 : 7. 1981. pp. 663-670

173. NANJUNDA SASTRY, N. 1962
"English in India." *Modern Review.* 112 : 6. pp. 474-476.

174. NARASIMHAIAH, Closepet Dasappa. 1964
"The English Language in India." *Hemisphere*(Australia) 8. April. pp. 26-30.

175. NARAYAN, R.K. 1964
"English in India". *IN* PRESS, J. (ed) : *Commonwealth Literature : Unity and Diversity in a Common Culture.* London, Heinemann Educational Books. pp. 120-124.

176. ——.1979
"English in India : The Process of Transmutation", *IN* NAIK, M.K. (ed) : *Aspects of Indian Writing in English*

177. NEHRU, Jawaharlal. 1963
"The Language Problem in India." *Bulletin, Central Institute of English.* 3. pp. 1-6. (The text of an address delivered extempore at the Central Institute of English, Hyderabad on July 22, 1963.)

178. NIGAM, Raghuvir Sahay. 1974
"The Library Language in University Education." *Educational Review.* 80 : 12. pp. 255-257.

179. NIHALANI, Narsu K. 1985
"English in the Third World : Changing Attitudes", *IN*

AMUR, G.S. *et. al.* (eds) : *Indian Readings in Commonwealth Literature.* New Delhi, Sterling. pp. 38-43.

180. *An Outline Report on the Position and Teaching of English in India.* 1966
Washington, D.C., Centre for Applied Linguistics.

181. PALIWAL, V.P. 1980
"English in India : Maid or Misteress ?" *Caravan.* 11. Jun. pp. 40-41.

182. PANDE, N.R.W. 1964
"English in India." *Triveni.* 33.October. pp. 68-75.

183. PANDIT, Prabodh B. 1975
"The Linguistic Survey of India—Perspectives on Language Use" *IN* OHANNESSIAN, S. *et. al.* : *Language Surveys in Developing Nations.* Arlington, Virginia, Centre for Applied Linguistics. pp. 71-86.

184. PANT, H, and CONNELL, P. 1980
English in India in the 1980s. New Delhi, British High Commission.

185. PARTHASARATHY, R. 1982
"All About Babu English." *Hindustan Times.* 24 Jan.

186. PATTANAYAK, Devi Prasanna. 1967
"English in India : A Reassessment." *NIE Journal.* 1 : 5 pp. 5-9.

187. —— 1970
Language Policy and Programmes. New Delhi, Ministry of Education and Youth Services.

188. PLATT, John T. ; WEBER, Heidi and HO, M.L. 1984
The New Englishes. London, Routledge and Kegan Paul. (Includes some pages on Indian English.)

189. PRASAD, Ila. 1978
"Literary Hangover From Colonial Days : Discussion." *CIEFL Newsletter*. 14 : 1. pp. 15-16. (A discussion on Indian English.)

190. PRIDE, John. (ed). 1982
New Englishes. Rowley, MA., Newbury.

191. PULLUM, G.K. 1971
"Indian Scripts and the Teacher of English." *English Language Teaching Journal*. 25 : 3. pp. 278-284.

192. PURKAYASTHA, K.M. 1968
"Indian English ?" *Century*. 17 Feb.

193. RAJADHYAKSHA, M.V. 1979
"Should English Go ?" *Illustrated Weekly of India*. 100 : 9. 4 Mar. pp. 6-9.

194. RAJAGOPALACHARI, C. 1962
The Question of English. Madras, Bharathan.

195. RAMA, R.P. 1971
" And Now 'Indish'." *Thought*. 6 Feb. p. 12.

196. RAMAN, A.S. 1974
"Mukherjee to Bannerjee." *London Magazine*. 14 : 3. Aug-Sep. pp. 117-123.

197. ——. 1977
"English After the English." *Sunday*. 30 Jan.

198. ——. 1978
"English in India." *Swarajya*. 22 : 51. 4 Jun. pp. 29-32.

199. RAO, B.N. 1980
"In Defence of Indian English." *Mirror*. 19 : 12. pp. 33-38.

200. RAO, R. 1978
"Caste of English India", *IN* NARASIMHAIAH, C. D.

(ed) : *Awakened Conscience : Studies in Commonwealth Literature.* Humanities Press. p. 420.

201, *Report of the Official Languages Commission, 1956*. 1957. New Delhi, Government of India Press.

202. RICE, F.A. (ed). 1962
Study of the Role of Second Languages in Asia, Africa and Latin America. Washington.

203. S.C. 1981
"English Language in India." *Frontier*. 13 ; 48. 25 Jul. pp. 6-9.

204. SAHGAL, Payan. 1972
"Seminar on Indian English--A Report." *Indian PEN.* 38 : 10. Oct. pp. 347-350.

205. SCRUTATOR (Pseudonym). 1962
In Defence of Good English. Calcutta, Writers Workshop.

206. SESHADRI, C. K. 1976-77
"English in India : A Historical Perspective." *Journal of the Maharaja Sayajirao University Baroda* (*Humanities*). 25 : 1—26 : 1. pp. 13-30.

207. SHARADA PRASAD, H.Y. 1986
"Coming Home." *Seminar*. 321. May. pp.23:26. (Special Issue on Indian English.)

208. SHARMA, Brij Bhushan. 1972
"Making English an Indian Tongue." *Times Weekly.* 26 Mar.

209. SHARMA, Promod Ban Bihari. 1970
Contrastive Study of Bhojpuri and English with special Reference to the Teaching of English. Thesis (Ph. D.)—Deccan College (Poona).

210. SHARMA, Ram. 1982
"Indian English for the Third World." *Hindustan Times.* 18 Jul.

211. SIDHANTA, N.K. 1965
"English Studies Today." *Bulletin, Central Institute of English.* 1. pp. 3-6.

212. SINGH, Bir. 1965
"Raising the Standards in English." *Indian Education.* 4 ; 1. pp. 16-18.

213. SINHA, Sidheshwardhari. 1983
"New Englishes." *Alok* (Bilingual Journal, Patna). 1 : 3 pp. 57-77.

214. SINHA, Surendra Prasad. 1978
English in India : A Historical Study With Particular Reference to English Education in India. Patna, Janki.

215. SPEIGHT, E.E. 1934
Indian Master of English. London, Longman.

216. SPENCER, John W. 1971
"Language Policies of the Colonial Powers and Their Legacies", *IN Current Trends in Linguistics.* V. 7. The Hague, Netherlands, Mouton. pp. 537-547.

217. SPITZBARDT, H. 1976
English in India. Saale, VEB Max Niemeyer verlag Halle

218. SRINIVASA IYENGAR, K.R. 1974
"English and English Studies in India." *The Journal of the Indian Writing English.* 2 : 1. pp. 13-18.

219. STEPHENSON, C. 1973
"Det Indo-Engelska Spraketsoch Litteratureus Wppkomst." *Bonniers Litera Magasin* (Stockholm). 42. pp. 251:261.

220. STILZ, Gerhard. 1982
Grundlagen Zur Literatur in Englischen Sprache : Indian. Munchen, Fink.

221. STOCQUELER, J.H. 1848
The Oriental Interpreter and Treasury of the East India Knowledge : A Companion to 'The Handbook of British India. London.

222. STREVENS, Peter D. 1964
"Varieties of English." *Englisches Studies.* 45. pp. 20-30.

223. ——. 1982
"World English and the World's Englishes—Or, Whose Language is it Anyway." *Journal of the Royal Society of Arts.* 5311, CXXX. pp. 418-431

224. SUBRAHMANIAN, K. 1972
"Seminar on Indian English." *CIEFL Newsletter.* 9-10. pp. 11-12.

225. TAMBIAH, S.J. 1967
"The Politics of Language in India and Ceylon." *Modern Asian Studies.* 1 : 3 pp. 215-240.

226. THADANI, J. 1978
"The Role of English in India." *English Around the World.* 18.

227. THAPER, Romesh. 1986
"The Problem." *Seminar.* 321. May. pp. 12-13. (Special Issue on Indian English.)

228. THAROOR, Shashi, 1985
"Indian English." *Illusrated Weekly of India.* 18-24 Aug pp. 14-15.

229. THUNDAY, Zacharias. 1976
"The Origins of Indian English." *Bulletin, Central Institute of English and Foreign Languages* (Hyderabad, India). 12. pp. 29-40.

230. TIRUMATESH, K.V. 1916
"Indian English : An Interlanguage Phenomenon." *The Hindu.* 7 Jan. p. 19.

231. TODD, Loveto, 1984
Modern Englishes : Pidgins and Creoles. Oxford, Basil Blackwell. (For Indian English, see pp. 38, 57-60, 72-73, 84, 86, 91.)

232. TRUDGILL, Peter and HANNAH, Jean. 1982
International English : A Guide to Varieties of Standard English. London, Edward Arnold. (For Indian English see pp. 7, 99-100, 102 and 104-111.)

233. TYRNER, A.G. 1966
"Indo-Anglian Literature and the Indian Elite." *The Cornell Journal of Social Relations.* 1 : 1. Spring. pp. 25-32.

234. UDAYA SHANKAR, P.N. 1982
"The Link Language of India—Why Not English", *IN* A.I.U.T.T.A. : *Collection of Papers Presented in the Fourteenth Conference — Seminar.* Annamalainagar, A.I.U.T.T.A. pp. 31-35.

235. UNIVERSITY OF DELHI. DEPARTMENT OF LINGUISTICS. 1985
National Seminar on Indian English, 15-16 Mar. (Cyclostyled papers and abstracts.)

236. VELAYUDHAN, S. 1982
"The English Language in India." *ELT Forum : Journal of English Studies.* 5 : 2. pp. 24-30.

237. VENKATESWARAN, R.J. 1985
"Role of English in India ." *Pioneer.* 15 Jun.

238. VERGHESE, Cherukothu Paul. 1970
"Indian English." *Indian Literature.* (New Delhi). 13 : 1 Mar.

239. VERMEER, Mira H. and VERMEER, Hans J. 1963
"Das Indo-Englische." *Lebende Sprachen.* 8. pp. 135-138. and 184.

240. VODDEN, M.H.D. 1962
"Some Suggestions for a new Syllabus for the Teaching of English in English-Medium Schools." *Teaching English.* 7 : 1, pp. 4-23.

241. VOHRA, D.B. 1982
"Why Not Indilish." *National Herald.* 16 Jul.

242. WADIA, A.R. 1954
The Future of English in India. Bombay, Asia Publishing House.

243. WASI, Muriel. 1978
"Indian English." *The Education Quarterly.* 22 : 2. pp. 20-21.

244. YADAV, R.K. 1966
The Indian Language Problem : A Comparative Study. Delhi.

3. LINGUISTIC ASPECTS

245. AGNIHOTRI, Rama Kant ; KHANNA, A.L. and MUKHERJEE, A. 1982
"Predictors of Achievement in English Tenses—A Sociopsychological Study." *Indian Journal of Applied Linguistics.* 8 : 2. pp. 89-105.

246. AGRAWAL, R.
The Nativization of English in India : Evidence From the Mass Media. Thesis (M.A.)—F.U. Berlin Englishes Seminar. (Unpublished).

247. ANNAMALAI, E. 1978
"The Anglicised Indian Languages : The Case of Code-Mixing." *International Journal of Dravidian Linguistics.* 7 : 2. pp. 239-247.

248. ————. 1986
"Bilingualism Through Schooling in India", *IN* ABBI, Anvita. (ed) : *Studies in Bilingualism.* New Delhi, Bahri. pp. 65-78.

249. ————. 1986
"Comment : Legal vs. Social." *International Journal of the Sociology of Language.* 60. pp. 145-156. (This is a Comment on the article by David F. Marshall 'The Question of an Official Language : Language Rights and the English Language Amendment.' There is a reference to the functional aspects of English in India.)

250. APTE, Mahadev L. 1970
"Some Sociolinguistic Aspects of Interlingual Communication in India." *Anthropological Linguistics.* 12 : 3.

251. ————. 1976
"Multilingualism in India and Its Socio-Political Implications : An Overview", *IN* O'BARR, William M. and O'BARR, Jean F. (eds) : *Language and Politics.* The Hague, Mouton. pp. 141-164.

252. ARJUNA, 1985
"Look at Butler English." *M.P. Chronicle.* 17 Jul.

253. ARYA, Ramesh Chandra. 1977
"Indian English—Is it Florid and Sentimental ? Discussion." *CIEFL Newsletter.* 13 : 4. p. 17.

254. ————. 1979
"The Identity of a Non-Native Model : The Case of Standard Indian English." *Indian Journal of Applied Linguistics.* 5 : 1. pp. 64-79.

255. ATWAL, Pritam S.
Using English Nationally and Internationally : A Course in Sounds and Syntax of English for Speakers of Modern Indic Languages. New Delhi, Kalyani.

256. BAL, Bijoy Kumar. 1981
L Interference in the Acquisition of English as L : An Exploration of the Special Problems Encountered by the Kondh Tribal Students of Orissa in Acquiring English. Thesis (M.Litt.)—Central Institute of English and Foreign Languages. (Unpublished.)

257. ————.
Sequence in L Syntax Acquisition—A Psycholinguistic Study of English Syntax Acquisition by Primary Level Oriya-Speaking Students. Thesis (Ph.D.)– Central Institute of English and Foreign Languages. (In Progress.)

258. BALASUBRAMONIAN, Brinda. 1987
"Language of Film Reviews in English Hindi and Tamil" *Language Forum.* 13. pp. 175-192.

259. BAXTER, Eunice H. 1984
"Evaluation of a Punjabi-English Language Programme for Primary School Children." *World Language English.* 4 : 1. pp. 36-39.

260. BAYER, Jennifer Mani. 1977
"Language Use in Five Domains of the Anglo-Indians in Mysore City." Paper presented at the All India Conference of Linguists, Muzaffarpur.

261. ————. 1980
A Sociolinguistic Investigation of the English Spoken by the Anglo-Indians in Mysore City. Thesis (Ph.D.)—Mysore University. (Published by the Central Institute of Indian Languages, Manasagangotri, Mysore in 1986.)

262. BHATIA, Sugam Chand. 1972
Comprehensibility of Educated Indian English and Its Implications in Curriculum and Pedagogy. Thesis (Ph.D.) —University of Texas, Austin.

263. ————. 1978
"Towards a Non-Native Standard in Indian English." *Indian Linguistics.* 39. pp. 225-232.

264. BUGHWAN, D. 1970
An Investigation Into the Use of English by Indians in South Africa With Special Reference to Natal. Thesis (Ph.D.)—University of South Africa, Pretoria. (Unpublished).

265. ————. 1975
"The English of Indians in Natal, South Africa." Paper delivered at the Linguistics Conference, University of Rhodesia, Salisbury, December.

266. CHATTERJEE, Kalyan Kumar. 1976
"Indian Engllsh : Problems of Identity." *Quest.* 99. pp. 57-60.

267. CHINNAKARN, Sanit. 1977
A Linguistic Analysis of English in Indian Advertisements. Thesis (M.A.)—University of Baroda, Baroda.

268. CHOUDHRY, Amitav. 1985
"The Evolution of Indian English ; Some Socio-Cultural and Psychological Considerations." Paper presented at the National Seminar on Indian English, Department of Linguistics, University of Delhi, 15-16 Mar.

269. DAS, Sisir Kumar, 1982
Indian English, *IN* PRIDE, J. (ed) : *New Englishes.* Rowley, Mass., Newbury House.

270. DASGUPTA, Probal. 1986
"On the Sociolinguistics of English in India." *Praci-Bhasha Vijnan, Indian Journal of Linguistics.* 13. pp. 61-88.

271. DASWANI, C.J. 1974-75
"Indian English." *Journal of the School of Languages, Jawaharlal Nehru University* (New Delhi). 2 : 2. pp. 34-49.

272. ————. 1978
"Some Theoretical Implications for Investigating Indian English", *IN* MOHAN, Ramesh. (ed) : *Indian Writing in English.* Madras, Orient Longman. pp. 115-128.

273. ————. 1981
Pidginization in a Multilingual Society : The Case of Indian English, *IN Proceedings of the 5th Congress of L'Association Internationale de Linguistique Applique Montreal, Aug. 1978.* Quebec, Les Presses De L'Universita Lavel. pp. 89-98,

274. DAVIDSON, T.T.L. 1969
"Indian Bilingualism and the Evidence of the Census of 1961." *Lingua.* 22 : 2-3. pp. 176-196.

275. DENISON, Norman. 1966
"The Nature and Diagnosis of Interference Phenomena (Largely English—Urdu)." *Philippine Journal for Language Teaching.* 4 : 3-4. pp. 1-16.

276. DESAI, B.T. 1982
A Linguistic Study of the English Elements in Kannada—English Code Switching. Thesis (Ph.D.)—Central Institute of English and Foreign Languages, Hyderabad.

277. DUA, Hans R. 1980
"Planning Language Use in Radio Broadcasts in a

Multilingual Country." *Indian Linguistics.* 41 : 1. pp. 1-9.

278. DUBEY, Vinod S. 1982
"Englishization in India : From Code-Mixing to Code-Intrusion." Paper presented at the 3rd International Conference on South Asian Languages and Linguistics, Central Institute of Indian Languages, Mysore.

279. DWIVEDI, R.K. 1970-71
"English in Indian Administration." *Bulletin, Central Institute of English.* 8. pp. 63-71.

280. FISHMAN, J.A., *et.al.* 1977
"English the World Over : A Factor in the Creation of Bilingualism Today", *IN* HORNBY, P.A. (ed) : *Bilingualism : Psychological, Social and Educational Implications.* New York, Academic Press. pp. 108-139.

281. FISHMAN, J.A., *et al.* (eds). 1977
The Spread of English, the Sociology of English as an Additional Language. Rowley, Mass., Newbury House.

282. GOVINDAN, A. 1976-77
Tamilian English : A Sociolinguistic Study. Annamalai, Annamalai University. (Unpublished Paper.)

283. GUMPERZ, John J. 1957
"Some Remarks on Regional and Social Language Differences in India", *IN* SINGER, M. (ed) : *Introducing India in Liberal Education.* Chicago.

284. GUMPERZ, John J. ; AGRAWAL, A. and AULAKH, Gurinder. 1977
Prosody, Paralinguistic and Contextualization in Indian English. Berkeley, Language Behaviour Research Laboratory, University of California. (Typescript.)

285. GUMPERZ, John J. and KALTMAN, Hannah. 1980
"Prosody, Linguistic Diffusion and Conversational Inference." *Proceedings of the Sixth Annual Meeting of the Berkeley Linguistics Society, 16-18 Feb.* pp. 44-65.

286. GUPTA, Anjuli.
"English in India—A Link Language for Whom ?" *IN* BETTINGER, Elfi and MEIER-FOHRBECK, Thomas. (eds) : *Von Shakespeare Bis Chomsky.* Frankfurt am Main, Verlag Peter Lang. pp. 285-302.

887. ————.
English in Indian Media. Thesis (Ph.D.)—Free University, Berlin. (In progress.)

288. GUPTA, Raghubir Saran. 1978
A Sociolinguistic Study of the Use of Mixed Hindi-English in Metropolitan Delhi. Thesis (D.Phil.)—York University, York. (Unpublished.)

289. GUPTA, Sagar Mal. 1977
Second Language Learning : A Process of Pidginization : Evidence From Indian English. Honolulu, East-West Centre, University of Hawaii. (Unpublished paper.)

290. GUTHRIE, Thomas Anstey.
Baboo Hurry Bungsho. Jabberjee, B.A.

291. HALSEG, M. 1972
"Uber Die Grundlage Der Rolle Der Englischen Sprache Der Genencsart in Gesellschaftlichen Leben Indiens in Der Gegen Wart (On the Basis of the Role Played by Present-Day English in the Social Life of Modern India)." *Mitteilungen des Institutes Fur Orientforschung Der Akademie Der Wissenschaften Der DDR Zu Berlin.* 17 : 3. pp. 383-392.

292. HAZARAT, Kallolini. 1978

"An Experiment in the Study of Multilevel Materials for Learning English." *Journal of the Gujarat Research Society* (Bombay). 40 : 1. pp. 26-32.

293. HOSALI, Priya. 1973
(a) *Hindi-English Code-Switching.* Thesis (M.A.)—University of Lancaster, Lancaster. (Unpublished.)

294. ————. 1982
Butler English : Form and Function. Thesis (Ph.D.)—Central Institute of English and Foreign Languages.

295. ————. 1984
"Butler English : How Pidgins Begin." Paper presented at an Inter-Collegiate Seminar Organized by the University College, London and the London School of Economics, 24 Oct.

296. ————. 1984
"Indian English." *TETE-A-TETE : An Interactive Newsletter of the Department of Correspondence Courses, Central Institute of English and Foreign Languages, Hyderabad.* 3 : 6-12. pp. 1-29.

297. ————. 1984
"Processes of Language Change in Butler English." Paper presented at the National Seminar held at Delhi University, Delhi, 2-4 Mar.

298. ————. 1984
"The Morphological Features of Butler English." Paper presented at the Sociolinguistics Symposium held at Liverpool, U.K., 7-9 Sep.

299. ————. 1985
"A Pidgin From India Called Butler English." Conference Lecture, University of Ottawa, Canada, Oct.

300. ————. 1986
"Butler English and Other Pidgins : A Comparison." Paper presented at the 6th Sociolinguistics Symposium, Newcastle on Tyne, U.K., 16-18 Apr. (Also appeared in : *CIEFL Working Papers in Linguistics.* 4 : 1. 1987. pp. 68-90.)

301. ————. 1986
"Standard English and Indian English." Paper presented at the 4th International Conference on the Teaching of English held at Carleton University, Ottawa, Canada, 11-16 May.

302. HOSALI, Priya and AITCHISON, Jean. 1986
"Butler English : A minimal Pidgin (?)" *Journal of Pidgin and Creole Linguistics.* 1 : 1. pp. 51-79.

303. Indian English : A Symposium on the Tribulations of a language in the Making. 1986 *Seminar.* 321. May.

304. IRULAPPAN, K.M. 1977
"Social Stratification of English Loan Assimilation in Tamil." Paper presented at the 7th All India Conference of Indian Linguists, Muzaffarpur.

305. JAMES, Gregory. 1979
"Some Aspects of Interlanguage : An Analysis of Some Features of a Tamil Speaker's English." *Indian Journal of Applied Linguistics.* 5 : 1. pp. 20-50.

306. "Jargon of the Vintage Butler." 1985
The Hindu. 5 May. p. 20.

307. KACHRU, Braj B. 1962
An Analysis of Some Features of Indian English : A Study in Linguistic Method. Thesis (Ph.D.)—University of Edinburgh. (Unpublished.)

308. ———. 1965
"The Indianness of Indian English." *Word.* 21 : 3. pp. 391-410.

309. ———. 1966
"Indian English : A Study in Contextualization", *IN* BAZELL, C.E., *et al.* (eds) : *In Memory of J.R. Firth.* London, Longman. pp. 255-287.

310. ———. 1969
"English in South Asia", *IN* SEBEOK, T. (ed) : *Current Trends in Linguistics.* Vol. 5. The Hague, Mouton. pp. 627-678.

311. ———. 1971
"English in India : A Pan-Indian and International Link." *English Around the World.* 4 May. pp. 1-2 and 4-7.

312. ———. 1971
"The Literary Heritage of Indian English." *The Hindustan Times Weekly.* 11 April. (A reply to Raja Ram Mehrotra's letter in the *Hindustan Times,* 7 Feb. 1971.)

313. ———. 1975
"The Englishization of Hindi : Language Rivalry and Language Change", *IN* RAUCH, I. and CARR, G.F. (eds) : *Linguistic Method : Papers in Honour of Herbert-Penzl.* The Hague, DeRidder Press. pp. 199-211.

314. ———. 1975
"Towards Structuring the Form and Function of Code-Mixing : An Indian Perspective." *Studies in the Linguistic Sciences.* 5 : 1. pp. 75-92.

315. ———. 1976
"Indian English : A Sociolinguistic Profile of a Trans-

planted Language." *Studies in Language Learning* (Unit for Foreign Language Study and Research, University of Illinois, Urbana). 2.

316. ————. 1976
"Models of English for the Third World : White Man's Linguistic Burden or Language Pragmatics ?" *TESOL Quarterly*. 10 : 2. pp. 221-239.

317. ————. 1977
"Linguistic Schizophrenia and Language Census : A Note on the Indian Situation." *Linguistics*. 186. pp. 17-32.

318. ————. 1977
"The New Englishes and Old Models." *English Language Forum*. 15 : 3. pp. 29-35.

319. KACHRU, Braj B. and SRIDHAR, S.N. (eds). 1978
"Aspects of Sociolinguistics in South Asia." *IJSL*. 16.

320. KACHRU, Braj. B. 1978
"Code-Mixing as a Communicative Strategy in India", *IN* ALATIS, James E. (ed): *Georgetown University Round Table on Languages and Linguistics 1978 : International Dimensions of Bilingual Education*. Washington, D.C., Georgetown University Press. pp. 107-124.

321. ————. 1978
English in South Asia, *IN* FISHMAN, J.A. (ed) : *Advances in the Study of Societal Multilingualism*. The Hague, Mouton. pp. 477-551. (Revised version.)

322. ————. 1978
"Indian English : A Sociolinguistic Profile of a Transplanted Language", *IN* KRISHNAMURTI, Bh. (ed) : *Introduction to Indian Languages and Linguistics*. New

Delhi, NBT. (Also in : *Studies in Language Learning.* 1 : 2. Spring 1976.)

323. ————. 1978
"Toward Structuring Code-Mixing : All Indian Perspective." *International Journal of the Sociology of Language.* 16. pp. 27-46. (A slightly revised version of his earlier paper with the same title published in *Studies in the Linguistic Sciences.* 5 : 1. 1975.)

324. ————. 1979
"Models of 'Non-Native English' : Origin, Development and Use." Paper presented at Conference on Progress in Language Planning : International Perspectives, New Jersey, 30 Apr.

325. ————. 1981
"American English and Other Englishes", *IN* FERGUSON, Charles A. and HEATH, Shirley (eds) : *Language in the USA.* New York, Cambridge University Press. pp. 21-43.

326. ————. 1981
"The Pragmatics of Non-Native Varieties of English", *IN* SMITH, Larry E. (ed) : *English for Cross-Cultural Communication.* London, Macmillan. pp. 15-39.

327. ————. 1982
"Introduction : English in South Asia", *IN* AGGARWAL, Narinder K. (compiler): *English in South Asia : A Bibliographical Survey of Resources.* Gurgaon, Indian Documentation Service. pp. IX-LXXX.

328. ————. 1982
Introduction : The Other Side of English, *IN* KACHRU, Braj B. (ed) : *The Other Tongue : English Across Cultures.* Urbana, Ill., The University of Illinois Press. pp. 1-12.

329. ————. 1982
"Meaning in Deviation : Toward Understanding Non-Native English Texts", *IN* KACHRU, Braj B. (ed) : *The Other Tongue : English Across Cultures.* Urbana, Ill., The University of Illinois Press. pp. 325-350.

330. ————. 1982
"Models for Non-Native Englishes", *IN* KACHRU, Braj B. (ed) : *The Other Tongue : English Across Cultures.* Urbana, Ill., The University of Illinois Press. pp. 31-57.

331. ————. (ed). 1982
The Other Tongue : English Across Cultures. Urbana, Ill,, The University of Illinois Press.

332. ————. 1982
"South Asian English", *IN* BAILEY, R.W. and GORLACH, M. (eds) : *English as a World Language.* Ann Arbor, University of Michigan Press. pp. 353-383.

333 ————. 1983
The Indianization of English : The English Language in India. New Delhi, Oxford University Press.

334. ————. 1983
"Models for New Englishes", *IN* COBARRUBIAS, Juan and FISHMAN, Joshua A. (ed) : *Progress in Language Planning.* The Hague, Mouton. pp. 144-170.

335. ————. 1983
"Normes Regionales de L'anglais", *IN* BEDARD, Edith and MAURAIS, Jacques, (eds) : *La Norme.* Quebec, Conseil de la Langue Francaise. pp. 707-730.

336. ————. 1984
"The Alchemy of English : Social and Functional Power of Non-Native Varieties", *IN* KRAMARAE, Cheris ;

SCHULZ, Muriel and O'BARR, William M. (eds) : *Language and Power*. Beverly Hills, Sage. pp. 176-193.

337. ————. 1984
"English as a Second Language", *IN* GREENBAUM, Sydney. (ed) : *The English Language Today*. Oxford, Pergamon Press.

338. ————. 1984
"Regional Norms for English'', *IN* SAVIGNON Sandra and BERNS, Margie S. (eds) : *Initiative in Communicative Language Teaching : A Book of Readings*. Reading, MA., Addison-Wesley. pp. 55-78.

339. ————. 1985
"Institutionalised Second Language Varieties", *IN* GREENBAUM, Sidney. (ed) : *The English Language Today*. Oxford, Pergamon Press. pp. 211-226.

340. ————. 1985
"Standards, Codification and Sociolinguistic Realism : The English Language in the Outer Circle," *IN* QUIRK, Randolph and WIDDOWSON, Henry G. (eds) : *English in the World : Teaching and Learning the Language and Literatures*. Cambridge, Cambridge University Press. pp. 11-30.

341. ————. 1986
The Alchemy af English : The Spread, Functions and Models of Non-Native Englishes. Oxford, PergamonPress.

342. ————. 1986
India, *IN* DEAR, I.C.B. (Compiler) : *Oxford English : A Guide to the Language*. Oxford, Oxford University Press. pp. 277-279.

343. ————. 1986
"The Indianization of English : The Imperial Transplant

of 1835 has Taken Root in the Soil of the Indian Sub-Continent and Flourishes Today as an Indian Language in its Own Right." *English Today*. No. 6. Apr.-Jun. pp. 31-33.

344. KACHRU, Yamuna. 1985
"Discourse Analysis, Non-Native Englishes and Second Language Acquisition Research." *World Englishes*. 4 : 2. pp. 223-232.

345. KALA, C.V. 1977
"Hybrid Conversational Malayalam : The Role of English in the Kerala Social Situation." *Anthropological Linguistics*· 19. pp. 265-273.

346. KARUNAKARAN, K. 1980
"Tamilian English; A Sociolinguistic Study", *IN* ISRAEL M. *et.al.* (eds) : *A Festschrift for Prof. M. Shanmugam Pillai*. Vol. 1. Madurai, Madurai Kamaraj University. pp. 283-292.

347. KATIKAR, Pratibha. 1985
The Meaning of the Modals in Indian English. Thesis (Ph.D.)—Shivaji University, Kolhapur.

348. KHUBCHANDANI, Lachman Mulchand. 1969
"Functional Importance of Hindi and English in India", *IN Language and Society in India*. Simla, Indian Institute of Advanced Study. pp. 178-189. (IIAS Transactions. 8.)

349. ————. 1 70
"English Bilingualism in India: A Sociolinguistic Study", *IN* LUGTON, R. (ed) : *English as a Second Language*. Philadelphia, Centre for Curriculum Development.

350. ————. 1973
"English in India : A Sociolinguistic Approach." *Inter-*

national Journal of Dravidian Linguistics. 2 : 2. pp. 199-211.

351. ———. 1973
"Indian Bilingualism and English : An Analysis of 1961 Census Data." *Demography-India.* (Delhi). 2 : 1.

352. ————. 1973
Indian Bilingualism and English : A Demographic Study. Simla, Indian Institute of Advanced Study. (Manuscript.)

353. ————. 1976
"English as a Contact Language in South Asia." *RELC Journal.* 7. pp. 21-30.

354. ————. 1976
"Language Factor in Census", *IN* VERDOODT, A. and KJOLSETH R. (eds) : *Language in Sociology.* Louvain, Peters. pp. 92-124.

355. ————. 1978
"Distribution of Contact Languages in India : A Study of the 1961 Bilingualism Returns", *IN* FISHMAN, Joshua A. (ed) : *Advances in the Study of Societal Multilingualism.* The Hague, Mouton. pp. 553-586.

356. ————. 1978
Language in a Modern Setting : Implications of Cultural Pluralism in Southern Asia.

357. ————. 1978
"Multilingual Education in India, *IN* SPOLSKY, Bernard and COOPER, Robert L. (eds) : *Case Studies in Bilingual Education.* Rowley, Mass., Newbury House. pp. 88-125.

358. KINDERSLEY, A.F. 1931
"Indian English, Its Development and Characteristics." *Transactions of the Philological Society.* p. 82.

359. KOTHANDARAMAN, R. 1968
Some Bilingual Observations With Special Reference to Tamil English Contact Situation. Thesis (M.A.)—Annamalai University, Annamalainagar.

360. KRISHNA MURTHY, D.R. 1982
"The Role of English in the Media", *IN* NRRASIMHAIAH, C.D. and SRINATH, C.N. (eds) : *English Its Contemporary Role in India.* Mysore, Dhvanyaloka. pp. 89-92.

361. KRISHNASWAMI, N. 1970
"Indian English : A Descriptive Study." *Pakha Sanjam.* 3 : 1-2. pp. 94-100.

362. KRISHNASWAMI, N. and AZIZ, Salim A. 1983
"Understanding Values, TEIL, and the Third World", *IN* SMITH, Larry E. (ed) : *Readings in English as an International Language.* Oxford, Pergamon. pp 95-101.

363. KRUSINA, A. 1966-67
"Indian English-Samostatna Varianta Anglictiny? (Indian English—An Independent Variety of English)" *Cizijazyky Ve Skole* (Praha). 10.

364. KUMAR, Ashok. 1982
Hindi-English Code-Switching in Academic Discourse. Thesis (M. Litt.)—Central Institute of English and Foreign Languages, Hyderabad.

365. ———. 1985
"Towards a Local Model of ELT in India : Evidence From Journalistic English." Paper Presented at a Seminar on English in the Mass Media held on 17-18 Aug. 1985 at the CIEFL, Hyderabad.

366. ———. 1986
"Certain Aspects of the Form and Functions of Hindi-

English Code-Switching." *CIEFL Working Papers in Linguistics.* 3-1. pp. 1-19. (Also appearing in : *Anthropological Linguistics* sometime in 1987).

367. ———. 1986
Certain Aspects of the Form and Function of Hindi-English Code-Switching. Thesis (Ph. D.)—Central Institute of English and Foreign Languages, Hyderabad.

368. ———. 1985
"Hindi-English Mixing in Scientific Discourse." *World Englishes.* 4 : 3. pp. 355-358.

369. LEITNER, Gerhard. 1983
"Indian English—A Critique of the Ethnography of Speaking." *International Journal of the Sociology of Language.* S4. pp. 153-167.

370. ———. 1984
"Indian English : A Critique of the Ethnography of Analysis", *IN Proceedings of the 13th International Congress of Linguists, Tokyo.*

371. LLAMZON, Teodoro A. 1983
"Essential Features of New Varieties of English", *IN* NOSS, R.B. (ed) : *Varieties of English in Southeast Asia.* Singapore, SEAMEO Regional Language Centre. pp. 91-109.

372. LOWENBERG, Peter H. 1986
"Non-Native Varieties of English." *Praci-Bhasha Vijnan Indian Journal of Linguistics.* 13. pp. 33-60.

373. LUTZE, Lothar. 1968
"Linguistic Prospects of the Emergence of an Internal Contact Language for India." *South Asian Studies.* 4.

374. MEHROTRA, Raja Ram. 1975
"Some Registral Features of Matrimonial Advertisement in Indian English." *English Language Teaching Journal.* 30 : 1. pp. 9-12.

375. ———. 1976
"Matrimonial Advertisment : A Study of Correlation Between Linguistic and Situational Features. A Sociolinguistic Analysis of Matrimonial Advertisements Published in *The Hindu* (Madras) and *The Hindustan Times* (Delhi). Also Examined as a Step Towards Indianization of the English Language." *Indian Institute of Advanced Studies, Occasional Papers, Studies in Lingulstics.* pp. 41-61.

376. ———. 1978
"Varieties of English : The Myth of Deviance." *English Teaching Forum.* 16 : 3. pp. 37-38.

377. ———. 1979
"Indian English : Some Myths and Misconceptions", *IN* SINHA, Krishna Nandan. (ed) : *Indian Writing in English.* New Delhi, Heritage. pp 195-205.

378. ———. 1982
"Indian English : A Sociological Profile", *IN* PRIDE, J. (ed) : *New Englishes.* Rowley, Mass., Newbury House. pp. 150-173.

379. ———. 1982
"International Communication Through Non-Native Varieties of English : The Case of Indian English", *IN* BRUMFIT, Christopher. (ed) : *English for International Communication.* Oxford, Pergamon Press. pp. 73-80.

380. ———. 1984
"Registral Features of Film Advertising in Indian English." *World Language English.* 3 : 3. pp. 160-163.

381. ———. 1985
"The Language of Buying and Selling Silk Goods", *IN* MEHROTRA, Raja Ram. *Sociolinguistics in Hindi Context*. New Delhi, Oxford & IBH. pp. 160-163.

382. ———. 1984
"Language of Film Advertising in Indian English." *World Language English.* 3 : 3. pp. 160-163.

383. ———. 1985
"The Language of Indian Writing in English : Some Sociolinguistic Evidence." Paper presented at the National Seminar on Indian English, Department of Linguistics, University of Delhi, 15-16 Mar. (To appear in : *English Worldwide* and in *English Across Cultures*. ed. by John Pride. The Hague, Mouton).

384. ———.
Indian English. Amsterdam, Benjamins. (Varieties of English Series.) (Forthcoming.)

385. ———.
Sociolinguistic Survey of Indian Pidgin English. (Tentative topic. Forthcoming.)

386. MISHRA, Arpita. 1980
"Discovering Connection." *Proceedings of the 6th Annual Meeting of the Berkeley Linguistics Society, 16-18 Feb*. pp. 73-89.

387. ——1985
Toward an Analysis of Conversation Management : A Cross Cultural Perspective. Thesis (Ph.D.)—Department of Anthropology, University of California, Berkeley. (Unpublished.)

388. ——. 1986
"Language abroad : A Sociolinguistic Study of Conver-

sations in Interethnic Settings", *IN* ABBI, Anvita. (ed) : *Studies in Bilingualism.* New Delhi, Bahri. pp. 79-103.

389. MOAG, R. 1982
"The Life Cycle of Non-Native Englishes", *IN* KACHRU Braj B. (ed) : *The Other Tongue: English Across Cultures* Urban, University of Illin is Press. pp. 270-288.

390. MOHAN, Jag. 1979
"Hindi Filmi English is Coming." *Verbatim.* 5 : 4. pp. 1-3.

391. MOHAN, Peggy. 1986
"Review of Braj B. Kachru's 'The Indianization English: The English Language in India." *Seminar.* 321. May. pp. 42-44. (Appeared earlier in 'Contributions to Indian Sociology, 1984.)

392. MUKAR, R.K. 1980
"Hindi-English Code-Mixing and Code-Switching." *10th International Conference of Dravidian Linguists, New* Delhi.

393. NARAYANASWAMI, V. R. 1980
"English in Indian Advertising", *IN Issues in Stylistics : Papers Presented at the Seminar on Stylistics Held at the Central Institute of English and Foreign Languages Hyderabad.* Hyderabad. CIEFL. pp. 197-212.

394. NELSON, Cecil L. 1982
"Intelligibility and Non-Native Varieties of English", *IN* KACHRU, Braj B. (ed) : *The Other Tongue : English Across Cultures.* Urbana, Ill., The University of Illinois Press. pp. 58·73.

395. ——. 1984
Intelligibility, the Case of Non-Native Varieties of English Thesis (Ph.D.)——The University of Illinois, Urbana, Ill. (Unpublished).

396. ——1985
"My Language, Your Culture" : Whose Communicative Competence ?" *World Englishes.* 4 ; 2. pp. 250-285

397. PANDIT, Ira. 1978
Some Aspects of Hindi-English Code Mixing and Code Switching. Thesis (M.A.)——University of York, York. (Unpublished.)

398. ——. 1979
"Some Formal and Pragmatic Aspects of Hindi-English Code Switching and Code Mixing." Paper presented at the 10th International Anthropological Congress, New Delhi.

399. ——. 1980
"Mixed Hindi English : The Emergence of a Distinct Code." Paper presented at the Dravidian Linguistic Association Decennial Celebration and Conference held at the University of Delhi, Delhi.

400. ——. 1980
"Some Observations on the Linguistic Status of Mixed Hindi-English : An Emerging Variety," *10th International Conference of Dravidian Linguists, New Delhi.*

401. ——. 1981
"Some Social Correlates of the Characteristic Patterns of usages of Mixed Hindi-English." *Indian Journal of Applied Linguistics.* 7. pp. 51-65.

402. ——. 1984
"Interaction of Topic and Characteristic Informal Intra Ground Verbal Behaviour of Urban Educated Speakers of Hindi." *Praci-Bhasha Vijyan, Indian Journal of Linguistics.* 11 : 1. pp. 1-7.

403. ——. 1986
Hindi-English Code Switching, Mixed Hindi-English. Delhi, Datta Book Centre.

404. PARASHER, S.V. 1979
Certain Aspects of the Functions and Form of Indian English : A Sociolinguistic Study. Thesis (Ph. D.)—Central Institute of English and Foreign Languages, Hyderabad.

405. ——. 1979
"Educated Indian Bilingual's Attitudes to English." *Indian Journal of Applied Linguistics.* 5 : 2. pp. 56-65.

406. ———. 1979
"Indian English : Model, Identity and Use." *Journal of Indian Education.* 5. pp. 68-75.

407. ——. 1979
"A Synchronic View of English Bilingualism in India." *CIEFL Bulletin.* 15 : 1. pp. 65-76.

408. ——. 1980
"Mother Tongue-English Diglossia : A Case Study of Educated Indian Bilingual's Language Use." *Anthropological Linguistics.* 22 : 4. pp. 151-162.

409. ——. 1981
"English in India : A Sociolinguistic Reappraisal." *Zeitschrift fur Anglistik und Amerikanistick.* 29. pp. 330-342.

410. ——. 1981
"Indian English ; A Sociolinguistic Perspective." *ITL : Review of Applied Linguistics.* 51, pp. 59-70.

411. PATHAK, R.S. 1982
"Bilingual Competence and Code-Mixing in India." *Indian Journal of Applied Linguistics.* 8 : 2. pp. 75-88.

412. PATNAIK, B.N. 1986
"On the Problem of Labelling Indian English." *Language Forum.* 12 : 1-2. (Forthcoming.)

413. PATTANAYAK, Devi Prasanna. 1969
Aspects of Applied Linguistics. Bombay, Asia Publishing (Chapter 6: English in India. pp. 41-48)

414. ― ―. 1978
"Some Observations on English in India : Its Form and Function", *IN* MOHAN, Ramesh. (ed) : *Indian Writing in English.* Madras, Orient Longman. pp. 184-191.

415. ― ― 1981
"Some Observations on English in India—Its Form and Function", *IN* PATTANAYAK, D.P. : *Multilingualism and Mother-Tongue Education.* Delhi, Oxford University Press. pp. 160-179. (Revised version).

416. PLATT, John T. 1977
"The Sub-Varieties of Singapore English ; Their Sociological and Functional Status", *IN* CREWE, W. (ed) ; *The English Language in Singapore.* Singapore, Eastern Universities Press. (Contains a discussion on English of Indians in Singapore.)

417. PLATT, John T. and WEBER, Heidi. 1980
English in Singapore and Malaysia : Status : Features : Functions. Kuala Lumpur, Oxford University Press. (Indian English : see pp. 9-14, 17 and 46.)

418. PRABHAKAR BABU, B.A. 1970-71
"Newspaper Headlines : A Study in Registral Features." *Bulletin, Central Institute of English.* 8. pp. 41-48.

419. PRATOR, Clifford. 1968
"The British Heresy in TESL", *IN* FISHMAN, Joshua A.; FERGUSON, Charles A and DASGUPTA, Jyotirindra(eds).: *Language Problems of Developing Nations.* New York, John Wiley and Sons. pp. 459:476. (This paper discusses the intelligibility of Indian English.)

420. RAY, Punya Sloka. 1969
The Economics For and Against English in India, *In*

Language and Society in India: Proceedings of a Seminar. Simla, Indian Institute of Advanced Study. pp. 118-121. (Transactions of the Indian Institute of Advanced Study. 8.)

421. ROSS, Aileen D. 1974
"The Attitude to English and Use of it by Students of Three Different Mother Tongues : Hindi, Kannada and Tamil." *Sociological Bulletin.* 23 : 2. pp. 224-235.

422. SADANAND, Kamlesh. 1983
The Use of English in Industries in Andhra Pradesh : A Sociolinguistic Study. Thesis (Ph. D,)—Central Institute of English and Foreign Languages, Hyderabad.

423. SAHGAL, Anju. 1983
A Sociolinguistic Study of the English Spoken by Delhi Elite. Thesis (M. Litt.)--University of Delhi, Delhi. (Unpublished.)

424. SAHGAL, Payan. 1972
"Swadeshi English." *Times Weekly.* 24 Dec.

425. SALUNKHE, Sumati. 1986
A Linguistic Study of Indian English Newspaper Headlines With Special Reference to Speech Reporting. Thesis (M. Phil.) — Shivaji University, Kolhapur.

426. SAPIR, R.P. 1974
"Desi English." *The Illustrated Weekly of India.* 31 Mar.

427. SARAF, R.S. 1970
"Educated Indian English : A Few Observations." *Progress of Education.* 45 : 4. pp. 125-128.

428. SCHUCHARDT, Hugo. 1980
"Indo-English", *IN* GILBERT, Glenn G. (ed). *Pidgin and Creole Languages*: *Selected Essays*, by Hugo Schuchardt. London, Cambridge University Press. (Originally published in : *Englische Studieu.* 15. 1891. pp. 286-305.)

429. SCIULLO, Anne-Marie Di : MUYSKEN, Picter and SINGH, Rajendra 1986.
"Government and Code-Mixing." *Journal of Linguistics.* 22. pp. 1-24. (There is a reference to Hindi-English Code-Mixing.)

430. SESHADRI, C.K. 1965
"British English and Indian English : A Linguistic Comparison." *Journal of the M.S. University of Baroda.* 14 : 1, pp. 17-27.

431. SHANMUGAM, R. 1980
"Some Problems of Bi-Cultural Linguistic Description of English, Tamil and Other Indian Languages", *IN* A.I.U. T.T.A. : *Collection of Papers Presented in the 12th Conference — Seminar.* Annamalainagar, A.I.U.T.T.A. pp. 115-119.

432. SHANTA. K.M. 1977
Code-Switching : Malayalam-English Form and Function. Thesis (M. Litt.)—Central Institute of English and Foreign Languages.

433. SHAPIRO, Michael C. and SCHIFFMAN, Harold F. 1981.
"Pidginization, Creolization and South Asian English", *IN Language and Society in South Asia.* Delhi, Motilal Banarsidas. pp. 194-214.

434. SHARMA, D.D. 1965-66
Some Problems of Translation—A Linguistic Comparison of Texts in English and Hindi. Thesis (Ph. D.)—University of Edinburgh, Edinburgh.

435. SHASTRI, S.V. 1978
The Structure of Non-Native EST. Lancaster, University of Lancaster. (Unpublished Research paper.)

436. SHASTRI, S.V. 1986
"Computers in English Language Research With Special Reference to Description of Indian English," *Focus on English.* 2 : 1. pp. 13-17.

437. SHASTRI, S.V.; PATIL KULKARNI, C.T. and SHASTRI, Geeta S. 1986
Manual of Information to Accompany the Kolhapur Corpus of Indian English for Use With Digital Computers Kolhapur, Department of English, Shivaji University. (Mimeographed.)

438. SHASTRI, S.V. 1987
"Code-Mixing in the Procress of Indianization of English." *Indian Linguistics.*

439. ——. 1983
"Towards a Definition of Indian English." *CIEFL Newsletter.* 28 : 3-4. pp. 1-8.

440. SHAW, Willard. 1979
English and the Indian Student Honolulu, East-West Centre, University of Hawaii. (Mimeographed.)

441. ——. 1981
"Asian Student Attitudes Towards English", *IN* SMITH, Larry E. (ed) : *English for Cross Cultural Communication* London, Macmillan. pp. 108-122.

442. SHUKLA, S.K. 1968
Problems of Translation and the Implications of Its Use as a Teaching Device with Special Reference to the Teaching of English to Hindi Speakers. Thesis (Research Diploma) —Central Institute of English, Hyderabad.

443. SINGH, Rajendra. 1985
"Grammatical Constraints on Code-Mixing : Evidence From Hindi-English." *Canadian Journal of Linguistics.* 30 : 1. pp. 33-45.

444. SINGH, V.D. 1980
"Review of Indian and British *English.*" *TESOL Quarterly.* 14 : 2.

445. ——. 1981
"Indian English : Search For an Independent Standard". *Naya Shikshak.* 23 : 3. pp. 73-79.

446. SINHA, Anjani Kumar. 1985
"May I Indulge in Indian English." Paper Presented at the National Seminar on Indian English, Department of Linguistics, University of Delhi. 15-16 Mar.

447. SINHA, Sidheshwar Dhari. 1981
"Indian English-Hinglish." *Alok* (SCERT, Patna). English Section. 1 : 2. pp. 1-6.

448. SISSON, Ralph Richard. 1969
"English and the Indian Linguistic Dilemma." *Today's Speech* (Kingston). 17 : 1. pp. 9-16.

449. SMITH, Larry E. and BISAZZA, John A. 1983
"The Comprehensibility of Three Varieties of English for Students in Seven Countries", *IN* SMITH, Larry E. (ed) : *Readings in English as an International Language.* Oxford, Pergamon Press. pp. 59-67.

450. SMITH, Larry E. and RAFIOZAD, Khalilullah. 1983
"English For Cross-Cultural Communication : The Question of Intelligibility", *IN* SMITH, Larry E. (ed). *Readings in English as an International Language.* Oxford, Pergamon Press. pp. 49-58.

451. SOOD, Vinay. 1985
"Things at Large : British or Indian ?" Paper presented at the National Seminar on Indian English, Department of Linguistics, University of Delhi, 15-16 Mar.

452. *S*outh Asian English. 1985
IN READER'S DIGEST ASSOCIATION : *The Right Word at the Right Time : A Guide to the English Language and How to Use It.* New York, Reader's Digest Association. pp. 580-582.

453. SPENCER, John. 1966
"The Anglo-Indians and Their Speech: A Socio-Linguistic Essay." *Lingua* 16, pp. 57-70.

454. SRIDHAR, Kamal Keskar. 1977
The Development of English as an Elite Language in the Multilingual Context of India : Its Educational Implications. Thesis (Ph.D.) — The University of Illinois.

455. ——. 1978
"English as the Language of Wider Communication in India", *IN* SRIVASTAVA, R.N. (ed) : *Vision of India.* New Delhi.

456. ——. 1979
"English in the Socio-Cultural Context in India." *Studies in Language Learning.* 2 : 2. pp. 63-79.

457. ——. 1982
"English in a South Indian Urban Context", *IN* KACHRU, Braj B. (ed) : *The Other Tongue : English Across Cultures.* Urbana, University of Illinois Press. pp. 141-153.

458. ——. 1982
"Functional Distribution of Hindi vis-a-vis Other Languages in South India." Paper presented at the South Asian Languages Roundtable Held at Syracuse University, 20-23 May.

459. SRIDHAR, Kamal Keshas. 1985
"Sociolinguistic Theories and Non-Native Varieties of English." *Lingua.* 68. pp. 85-104.

460. SRIDHAR, Kamal Keskar and SRIDHAR, S.N. 1986
"Bridging the Paradigm Gap : Second Language Acquisition Thory and Indigenized Varieties of English." *World Englishes.* 5 : 1. pp. 3-14.

461. SRIDHAR, S.N. 1978
"On the Functions of Code-Mixing in Kannada." *International Journal of the Sociology of Language.* 16. pp. 109-107. (Discusses the Mixing of English and Kannada.)

462. ——.
"The Anatomy of Deviation : Toward a Syntactic Typology of Non-Native Englishes." (Forthcoming.)

463. SRINIVASA VARMA, G. 1982
"Interference of Tamil in English." *Pakha Sanjam.* 15. pp. 579-584.

464. SRIVASTAVA, R.N. 1985
"Perspectives on the Study of Indian English." Paper presented at the National Seminar on Indian English, Department of Linguistics, University of Delhi, 15-16 Mar.

465. STREVENS, Peter. 1982
"The Localized Forms of English, *IN* KACHRU, Braj B. (ed) : *The Other Tongue* : *English in Non-Native Context* Urbana, University of Illinois Press. pp. 33-30.

466. SUBRAHMANIAN, K. 1978
"My Mrs. is Indian." *Anthropological Linguistics*. 20 : 6 pp. 295-296.

467. THORPE, Michael. 1981
"Some English Reactions to Indian English." *Literary Half-Yearly*. 22 : 1. pp. 94-100.

468. TICKOO, Asha Kiran. 1979
Indian English: An Approach to a Fundamental Theoretical Conceptualization. Thesis (M. Litt.)—— Central Institute of English and Foreign Languages, Hyderabad.

469. TRIVEDI, H.C. 1965.
A Study of an Indian English Translation of a Gujarati Short Story, Edinburgh, Department of Applied Linguistics, University of Edinburgh. (Unpublished Diploma paper.)

470. ULLRICH, Helen E. 1982
"Rural and Urban Multilingualism : A South Indian

Case." *International Journal of the Sociology of Language.* 34. pp. 25-50.

471. VAID, Jyotsna. 1980
"The Form and Function of Code-Mixing in Indian Films : The Case of Hindi and English." *Indian Linguistics.* 41 : 1. pp. 37-44.

472. VALENTINE, Tamara M. 1985
"Cross-Sex Conversation in Indian English Fiction." *World Englishes.* 4 : 3. pp. 319-332.

473. VARMA, Ravi S. 1980
"Pidiginisation in English-Hindi Contact Situation." 10th International Conference of Dravidian Linguistis. New Delhi.

474. VENKATA REDDY, K. 1983
"Towards Indian English." *Triveni.* 52 : 2, pp. 51-54.

475. VERGHESE, Cherukothu Paul. 1969
"Problems of the Indian Translator in English." *Indian Literature.* 12 : 1. pp. 86-93. (Also reprinted in his book, *Essays on Indian Writing in English.* New Delhi, N.V. Publications, 1975. Chap. 4, pp. 14-20.

476. ——. 1973
"Indish or English." *Times of India.* 21 Jan. (Also reprinted in his book, *Essays on Indian Writing in English.* New Delhi, N.V. Publications. 1975. pp. 8-13.

477. VERMA, Manindra Kishore. 1962
"Teaching English to Speakers of Hindi. (1) The Approach." *Language Learning.* 12 : 4. pp. 273-280.

478. ——. 1976
The Impact of English : A Sociolinguistic Study of the Indian Situation. York, University of York. (Unpublished paper.)

479. VERMA, Shivendra Kishore. 1972
"A Linguist's View of English in India." *Indian and Foreign Review.* 10-15 Oct.

480. ——. 1973
"Hindi-English Code-Switching." Paper presented at the Workshop on Social Stratification and Language Behaviour at the Indian Institute of Advanced Study, Simla, 5-12 May.

481. ——. 1975
"Code-Switching : Hindi-English." *ITL. : Review of Applied Linguistics.* 28. pp. 35-48.

482. ——. 1976
"Code-Switching : Hindi-English." *Lingua.* 38 : 2. pp. 153-165.

483. ——. 1982
"Politeness in Indian English : An Exploration in the Functions of Language." *Praci-Bhasha Vijnan Indian Journal of Linguistics.* 9 : 2. pp. 26-40.

484. ——. 1985
"Language Modernization: Explorations in the Dcvelopment of Registers." *International Journal of Dravidian Linguistics.* 14 : 1. pp. 1-16.

485. VERMEER, Hans Josef. 1971
'Indisch' Boy, *IN* SCHMITT-BRANDT, Robert. (ed) : *Donum Indogermanicum. Festgafe fur Anton Scherer (On the Occasion of His 70th Birthday).* Heidelberg. pp. 70-81.

486. VISWANATHAM, Kalive. 1978
"Englishes and Standard Englishes", *IN* MANUEL, M. and AYYAPPA PANIKER, K. (eds) : *English and India* Madras, Macmillan. pp. 172-180.

487. WEINREICH, Uriel. 1957
"Functional Aspects of Indian Bilingualism." *Word.* 13 : 2. pp. 203-233.

488. WIDDOWSON, H.G. 1977
Pidgin and Babu, *IN* CORDER, S. Pit. and ROULET, E.T.E. (eds) : *The Notion of Simplification, Interlanguages and Pidgins and Their Relation to Second Language Pedagogy*. Neuchatel, Universita De Neuchatel. pp. 163-170.

489. WONG, Irene. 1982
Native-Speaker English for the Third World Today? *IN* PRIDE, J.B. (ed) : *New Englishes*. Rowley, M.A., Newbury House. pp. 259-286.

490. YARDI, V.V. 1978
"English as a Non-Native Language : Need for Defining Its Status." *Newsletter, Central Institute of English and Foreign Languages*, Hyderabad. 14 : 1. pp. 10-14.

4. LEXICONS

491. BARRERE, A.M.V, and LELAND, C.G. 1889-1890
A Dictionary of Slang, Jargon and Cant (English/American and Anglo-Indian). Edinburgh.

492. BROWN, C. Ph. 1852
The 'Zillah' Dictionary in the Roman Character, Explaining the Various Words Used in Business in India. Madras Printed by D.P.L.C. Connor Society's Press.

493. CARNEGY, Patrick. 1877
Kachahari Technicalities : A Glossary of Terms, Rural, Official and General in Daily Use in the Courts of Law

and in Illustration of the Tenures Customs, Arts and Manufactures of Hindustan. 2nd ed. Allahabad, Printed at the Allahabad Mission Press.

494. ELLIOTT, H.M. 1845
Supplement to the Glossary of Indian Terms. Agra.

495. *Glossary of Indian Terms Containing Many of the Most Important and Useful Indian Words Designed for the Use of Officers of Revenue and Judicial Practitioners and Students.* 1877. Madras.

496. HAWKINS, R.E. 1976
Oxford Dictionary. A Supplement of Indian Words. IN The Little Delhi, Oxford University Press.

497. ——. (compiler and ed). 1984
Common Indian Words in English. Delhi, Oxford University Press.

498. *Indian Vocabulary to Which Prefixed the Forms of Impeachment-* 1988. Stockdale.

499. LENTZNER, K. 1891
Worterbuch der Englischen Volkssprache Australiens Einiser Englischer Mischsprachen. Halle, Leipzig.

500. ——. 1891
Colonial English : A Glossary of Australian, Anglo-Indian Pidgin English, West Indian and South African Words. London, Kegan Paul.

501. MORRIS, E.E. 1864
Austral English : A Dictionary of Australasian Words, Phrases and Usages. London.

502. NIHALANI, Paroo. ; TONGUE R.K. and HOSALI, Priya. 1978
Indian and British English : A Handbook of Usage and Pronunciation. Delhi, Oxford University Press.

503. ROBERTS, T.T. 1800
An Indian Glossary, Consisting of Some Thousand Words and Forms Commonly Used in the East Indies. London, Murray and Highley.

504. ROEBUCK, Thomas (Captain). (compiler). 1882
A Laskari Dictionary or Anglo-Indian Vocabulary of Nautical Terms and Phrases in English and Hindustani, originally compiled by Captain Thomas Roebuck. Revised and corrected by William Carmichael Smyth. Re-edited and enlarged by George Small. London, W.H. Allen.

505. WHITWORTH, George C. 1885
An Anglo-Indian Dictionary. London, Kegan Paul.

506. WILSON, H.H. 1842
Glossary of Indian Terms. (A preliminary edition.)

507. ——. 1855
A Glossary of Judicial and Revenue Terms and of Useful Words Occurring in Official Documents, Relating to the Administration of British India. London, W.H. Allen (Enlarged edition by A.C. Ganguli and N.D. Basu. Calcutta, Eastern Law House, 1940.)

508. YULE, Henry and BURNELL, A.C. 1966
Dictionary of Indian English, edited by G.B.T. Kurian. Madras, Indian Universities Press.

509. ——. 1886
Hobson-Jobson :A Glossary of Colloquial Anglo-Indian Words and Phrases and of Kindered Terms, Etymological Historical, Geographical and Discursive. London, (New edition edited by William Crooke. Published by John Murray, 1903.)

510. ——. 1985
Hobson-Jobson : A Glossary of Colloquial Anglo-Indian Words and Phrases and of Kindered Terms, Etymological

Historical Geographical and Discursive. 2nd ed. Edited by William Crooke. New Edition with a New Foreword by Anthony Burgess. London, Routledge and Kegan Paul.

5. LEXIS AND VOCABULARY

511. ALAM, Qaiser Zoha. 1975
"A Lexical Feature of Newspaper English in India." *Indian Linguistics.* 36. pp. 29-36.

512. ———. 1983
"A Lexical Feature of Newspaper English in India", *IN* ALAM, Qaiser Zoha : *Issues : Linguistic and Pedagogic.* New Delhi, Sterling. pp. 25-35. (Slightly revised version of his 1975 paper.)

513. ANNAMALAI, E. 1971
Lexical Insertion in a Mixed Language," *IN Papers From the Seventh Regional Meeting of the Chicago Linguistic Society, 16-18 Apr.* pp. 20-27.

514. ARUMUGASWAMI, T. 1881
Inglishum Tamirumagiya Okkabuleniyam Daiyalagsum (*English-Tamil Vocabulary. Tamilised English*). Madras.

515. BARANNIKOV, P.A. 1968
"Hindi Shabdaavali Me Angrezi Se Aye Shabdo Kaa Sthaan. (Place of English Loan Words in Hindi Lexicon)-" *Nagari Pracharini Patrika.* 63. pp. 357-366.

516. BHATIA, Kailash Chandra. 1959
"Hindi me Angrezii se Aagat Shabdo Kaa Bhaasaa Taatvik Adhyayan. (A Linguistic Study of the English Loan Words in Hindi.)" *Bharatiya Sahitya.* 4 : 1. pp. 37-42.

517. BHIDE, Hari Sadashiv. 1949
A Study in the Development of English Vocabulary Since 1930. Thesis—Bombay University, Bombay.

518. CRAIGIE, W.A. 1954
"Introductory Note", *IN* SUBBA RAO, G. : *Indian Words in English : A Study in Indo-British Cultural and Linguistic Relations.* Oxford, Oxford University Press.

519. DUSTOOR, Phiroze Edulji. 1968
The World of Words. Bombay, Asia Publishing House. (Includes chapters on Indian English.)

520. FOSTER, W. 1900
"Some Anglo-Indianisms." *Indian Antiquary.* 29. p. 408.

521. HEDBERG, J. 1941-42
"Some Hindustani Designations of British Officials." *SN Ph.* 14. pp. 340-342.

522. JAYAPAL, Maya. 1984
A Study of Some Lexical Items in Contemporary Indian English. Thesis—Regional English Language Centre, Singapore. (Unpublished. No. RELC/In/102/1.)

523. KACHRU, Braj B. 1973
"Toward a Lexicon of Indian English", *IN* KACHRU, Braj B. and LEES, Robert B. (eds): *Issues in Linguistics: Papers in Honour of Henry and Renee Kahane.* Urbana, University of Illinois Press. pp. 352-376.

524. ———. 1975
"Lexical Innovations in South Asian English." *International Journal of the Sociology of Language.* 4. pp. 55-94. (Revised version of his earlier paper.)

525. ———. 1978
"Lexical Innovations in South Asian English", *IN* MOHAN, Ramesh. (ed) : *Indian Writing in English.* Madras, Orient Longman. pp. 80-100.

526. ———. 1980
"The New Englishes and Old Dictionaries in Lexicographical Research on Non-Native Varieties of English", *IN* ZGUSTA, Ladislav. (ed) : *Theory and Method in Lexicography : Western and Non-Western Perspectives.* Columbia, S.C., Hornbeam Press. pp. 71-101.

527. LIMAYE, Mohan R. 1966
"Towards a Better English-Marathi Dictionary." *Journal of the S.N.D.T. Women's University.* 1. pp. 62-90.

528. MILLS, J.V.G. 1975
"Ma Huan's Contribution to the Hobson-Jobson of Yule and Burnell (English-Indian Slang." *T'Oung PAO.* 61 : 1-3. pp. 148-160.

529. PRIUTZ, W. 1933
"Anglo-Indisch Cheroot Zigarre." *Zeitschrift Der Deutschen Morgenlandischen Gesellschaft* (Wiesbaden). 86.

530. SERJEANTSEN, M.S. 1961
A History of Foreign Words in English. New York, Barnes and Noble. (See chapter X.)

531. SHASTRI, S.V. 1978
English Word Meanings and Their American and Indian Variants—A Study of Six Lexical Items. Thesis—University of Lancaster, Lancaster. (Unpublished.)

532. ———. 1980
"A Computer Corpus of Present Day Indian English." *ICAME News* (Bergen, The Norwegian Computing Centre for the Humanities). 4. pp. 9-10.

533. ———. 1985
"Towards a Description of Indian English : A Standard Corpus of Indian English in Machine-Readable Form." *English World-Wide.* 6 : 2.

534. ———. 1985
"Word Frequencies in Indian English : A Preliminary Study." *ICAME News* (Bergen, The Norwegian Computing Centre for the Humanities). 9. pp. 38-44.

535. SINCLAIR, W.F. 1889
"Indian Names for English Tongues." *Journal of the Royal Asiatic Society of Great Britain and Ireland* (New Series). 21. pp. 159-178.

---

6. BORROWINGS, LOANS AND INFLUENCES

(English—Indian Languages and Indian Languages—English)

---

536. AKKIREDDY, S. 1971
English Loan Words in Telugu. Thesis (Ph. D.)—Sri Venkateswara University, Tirupathi.

537. ANNIAH GOWDA, H.H. 1954
The Influence of English on Indian Languages With Particular Reference to Kannada. Aligarh. (Manuscript).

538. BAILEY, T.G. 1928-30
"English Words in Punjabi." *Bulletin of the School of Oriental and African Studies.* v. 4. pp. 783-790 and v. 5. pp. 234-250.

539. BARANNIKOV, P.A. 1958
"Hindi Sabdavali Men Angreji se ae Sabdon ka Sthana. (The Place of English Loan Words in Hindi.)" *Nagari Pracharini Patrika.* 63. pp. 357-366.

540. BHATIA, Kailash Chandra. 1957
"Angrezi (t) aur (d) tatha Hindi Mem Unake Vibhinna

Rupa. (The Realization of English (t) and (d) in Hindi.)" *Bharatiya Sahitya.* Jan.

541. ———. 1957
"Hindi me Angrezii se Grahit Mishr Shabd (Mixed Words Borrowed From English Into Hindi.)" *Bharatiya Sahitya.* 2 : 3. pp. 109-114.

542. ———. 1959
Hindi Mem Angreji ke Agata Sabdom ka Bhasha Tattvika Adhyayana. (A Linguistic Study of English Loan Words in Hindi.) Thesis (Ph. D.)—Agra University, Agra. (Published in 1967 by Hindustani Akademy, Allahabad.)

543. BHATIA, Tej K. 1982
"English and the Vernaculars of India : Contact and Change." *Applied Linguistics.* 3 : 3. pp. 235-245.

544. BHATTACHARYYA, D.C. 1964
"The Impact of English Borrowings on the Bengali Language." *Calcutta Review.* 172. Jul. pp. 49-56.

545. CHANDOLA, Anoop Chandra. 1963
"Some Linguistic Influences of English on Hindi." *Anthropological Linguistics.* 5 : 2. pp. 9-13.

546. CHIDAMBARANATH CHETTIAR, A. 1964
"Indian Words in English Dictionary." *Annals of Oriental Research.* 19 : 2. pp. 1-11.

547. DHAR, K.L. 1963
"English Loan Words in Hindi." Leeds, University of Leeds. (Unpublished paper.)

548. ————. 1966
"Some Semantic Features of English Loan-Words in Hindi." *Teaching English.* 9 : 1. April.

549. DIL, Afia. 1966
English Loan-Words in Bengali, *IN Pakistani Linguistics (Shahidullah Presentation Volume)*. pp. 185-242.

550. GEORGE, K.M. 1978
Influence of English on the Structure of Malayalam, *IN* MANUEL, M. and AYYAPPA PANIKER, K. (eds) : *English and India.* Madras, Macmillan. pp. 221-230.

551. GHATE, Rhona. 1969
"Indian Words in English." *Illustrated Weekly of India.* 90 : 26: 29 Jun. p. 45.

552. INDURKHYA, B.L. 1961
"A Study of English-Hindi Loan Words." *CIEFL Bulletin.* 1. pp. 132-133.

553. IRVINE, W. 1900
"Notes on Some Anglo-Indian Words." *Indian Antiquary.* 29. pp. 270-272 and 361-363.

554. JHAVERI, Bipin. 1971
"Indian Words in English." *Indian Writing Today.* 5 : 4. pp. 215-218.

555. KALEEM, Nafeesa. 1981
English Loan-Words in Tamil : An Ethno-Semantic Study. Thesis (Ph.D.)—Central Institute of English and Foreign Languages.

556. KOSHAL, Samyukta. 1978
Conflicting Phonological Patterns : A Study in the Adoption of English Loan Words in Hindi. Chandigarh. Bahri.

557. KUMAR, V.S. 1965
"The Influence of English on Indian Languages." *Modern Review.* 117 : 1. pp. 71-75 and 117 : 5. pp. 374-377.

558. KHUSHWANT SINGH. 1986
"Bagarap Longo." *Sunday*. 13 : 48. 19-25 Oct. p. 7. (Samples of Pidgin Indian English and borrowing of English words into Punjabi are given.)

559. MAHATO, Pashupati. 1974
A Linguistic Study of English Loan-Words in Rabindra Literature. Calcutta, Mahato.

560. MASTER, A. 1939-42
"Some English Loan-Words in Gujrati." *Bulletin of the School of Oriental and African Studies*. 10. pp. 25-30.

561. MISRA, V.N. 1963
Hindi Bhasha Aura Sahitya Para Angreji Prabhava, 1870-1920. (The Influence of English on Hindi Language and Literature, 1870-1920.) Dehradun, Sahitya Sadan.

562. MYLERU, G.R. 1952
"Some Dravidian Loan Words in English." *Tamil Culture*. 1 : 2. pp. 143-153.

563. NADARAJAN, Vimala. 1983
"English Loan Words in Tamil Journals", *IN* PATTANAYAK. D.P. and ANNAMALAI, E. (eds) : *To Greater Heights : Faculty Research of CIIL, 1969-1979. Part II.* Manasagangotri, Mysore, Central Institute of Indian Languages. pp. 467-477,

564. PATHAK, Ganga Prasad. 1975
"Angrezii Bhaasaao me Prayukt Hindi Shabd. (Hindi Words Used in English Language.)" *Bhasha : Vishv Hindi Sammelan Ank*. pp. 50-60.

565. PATNAIK, B.N. and PANDIT, Ira. 1986
"Englishization of Oriya", *IN* KRISHNAMURTHY, Bh. (ed) : *South Asian Languages Structure and Convergence Diglossia*. New Delhi, Motilal Banarsidas. pp. 232-243.

566. PATNAIK, B.N. 1986
"On the Persistence of Borrowed Forms in Language. (A Study of the Englishization of Oriya at the Level of

Linguistic Etiquette.)" *International Journal oj Dravidian Linguistics.* 15 : 1. pp. 119-137.

567. SAGERT, H. 1951
Indisches Wortgut in Englischen, (Indian Words in English.) Thesis (Ph.D.)—Berlin. (Unpublished.)

568. SHANMUGAM PILLAI, M. 1968
"English Borrowings in Educated Tamil', *IN* KRISHNAMURTHY, Bh. (ed) : *Studies in Indian Linguistics.* Annamalainagar, Centre of Advanced Study in Linguistics. pp. 296-306.

569. SUBBARAO, G. 1947
Indian Loan Words in English : A Study in Anglo-Indian Cultural and Linguistic Relations From 1600 till the Present Day. Thesis (Ph.D.)—Madras University, Madras.

570. ————. 1954
Indian Words in English : A Study in Indo-British Cultural and Linguistic Relations. London, Oxford University Press.

571. SURESH, J. 1980
"Some English Loan Words in Kadar", *IN* A.I.U.T.T.A.: *Collection of Papers Presented in the 12th Conference-Seminar.* Annamalainagar, A.I.U.T.T.A. pp. 196-201.

572. THYAGARAJU, A.F. 1933-34
"English Loan Words in Modern Telugu." *Quarterly Journal of the Mythic Society.* pp. 171-175.

573. TUCKER, Chandran. 1986
A Dictionary of English Loan-Words in Modern Tamil. New Delhi, Biblia Impex.

574. TUFAIL, Muhammad. 1960
The Shift in Meaning of English Loan Words in Urdu. Thesis (Diploma)—School of Applied Linguistics, University of Edinburgh, Edinburgh. (Unpublished.)

575. UMAROVA, Barno and KHAN, Majida. 1986
"Indian Loan-Words of Medieval Period in English." *International Journal of Dravidian Linguistics.* 15 : 1. pp. 24-34.

576. VARMA, Dhirendra. 1932
English Loan Words in Hindi. Allahabad, University of Allahabad.

577. VARMA, Ravi S. 1972
"A Note on Phonological Substitution in English Loan Words in Hindi." *Indian Linguistics.* 33. pp. 169-173.

578. ————. 1974
"English Loan Words in Hindi : A Study in Semantic Change." *Modern Review.* 134 : 2. pp. 100-107.

579. ————. 1978
"English Loan-Words in Hindi", *IN* KELKAR, Ashok R. *et al.* (eds): *Proceedings of the All-India Conference of Linguists.* Poona, Linguistic Society of India. pp. 311.

580. ————. 1981
Linguistic Restructuring of English Loan Words in Hindi. Thesis (Ph.D.)—Rajasthan University, Jaipur.

581. ————. 1984
"Creative Use of English Loan Words in Hindi." *Gaveshana.* 43. pp. 77-82.

582. VENUGOPALACHARYA, S. 1984
English, Greek and Latin Words of Kannada-Tamil Origin. Ashoka Nagar, Mandya, the Author.

583. VEST, E.B. 1948
"Native Words Learned by American Soldiers in India and Burma in World War II." *American Speech.* 23. pp. 223-231.

7. PHONETICS AND PHONOLOGY

584. ABDUL GHAFFAR KHAN. 1974-75
A Study of the Spoken English of Manipuri (Meitei) Students at the Pre-Degree Level and Remedial Exercises Based on the Study. Thesis (Diploma)—Central Institute of English and Foreign Languages, Hyderabad.

585. AGARWAL, K.K 1973
A Comparative Study of English and Hindi Intonation. Thesis (Research Diploma)—Central Institute of English and Foreign Languages, Hyderabad.

586. AGNIHOTRI, Rama Kant and SAHGAL, Anju. 1985
"Is Indian English Retroflexed and R-Full?" *Indian Journal of Applied Linguistics.* 11 : 1. pp. 97-108.

587. AHMAD, Munir. 1963-64
A Contrastive Phonological Study of English and Urdu With Special Reference to Some Major Problems of Pronunciation. Bangev, Department of Linguistics, University of North Wales. (Unpublished paper.)

588. ALI, Asad. 1978
A Description of the Segmental Phonemes of the English Spoken by Urdu Speakers. Thesis (M.Litt.)—Delhi University. Delhi.

589. ————. 1980
A Phonological and Syntactic-cum-Stylistic Description of English Spoken by the Urdu Speakers of North India. Thesis (Ph.D.)—Delhi University, Delhi.

590. ALI, Ashraf. 1967
The Sounds of English and Bengali. Thesis (Diploma)—Welsh College of Advanced Technology, Bangev. (Unpublished.)

591. ANANTHAM, Sundur. 1959
A Study of the Pronunciation Problems Involved in the Teaching of English to Telugu Speakers. Thesis (Ph.D.)—University of Michigan, Michigan.

592. APPARAO, M. 1978
Orthography as Underlying Representation : A Study of R.P. and Telugu English Within the Framework of Generative Phonology. Thesis (M.Litt.)—Central Institute of English and Foreign Languages, Hyderabad.

593. ASIF NISAR. 1972
Pronunciation Difficulties of Hindi-Urdu Speaking Learners of English. Thesis (M.Phil.)—Aligarh Muslim University, Aligarh.

594. ————. 1973
A Contrastive Analysis of Urdu/Hindi and English Sounds. Thesis (M.Phil.)—Aligarh Muslim University, Aligarh.

595. BALAGOPAL, N. 1978
A Remedial Course in English Plosives for Malayalam Speakers. Thesis (Post-graduate Diploma)—Central Institute of English and Foreign Languages, Hyderabad. (Unpublished.)

596. BALASUBRAMANIAN, T. 1972-73
"The Vowels of Tamil and English—A Study in Contrast." *Bulletin, Central Institute of English and Foreign Languages.* 9. pp. 27-34.

597. ————. 1975
"Stress and Rhythm in English and Tamil—A Study in Contrast." *Bulletin, Central Institute of English and Foreign Languages.* 11. pp. 1-13.

598. ————. 1981
A Textbook of English Phonetics for Indian Students. Madras, Macmillan India.

599. BANSAL, Ram Krishna. 1962
"A Study of the Vowel System of Indian English as Spoken by Educated Hindi Speakers in Delhi, East-Punjab and West Uttar Pradesh." *Bulletin, Central Institute of English.* 2. pp. 27-32.

600. ————. 1966
The Intelligibility of Indian English—Measurements of the Intelligibility of Connected Speech and Sentence and Word Materials, Presented to Listeners of Different Nationalities. Thesis (Ph.D.)—University of London, London.

601. ————. 1966-67
"Spoken English in India, Suggestions for Improvement." *Bulletin, Central Institute of English.* 6. pp. 95-116.

602. ————. 1966-67
"A Study of the Intonation Patterns in Educated Indian English." *Bulletin, Central Institute of English.* 6. pp. 117-122.

603. ————. 1969
The Intelligibility of Indian English. Hyderabad, Central Institute of English. (Monograph No. 4.)

604. ————. 1971
"Better Spoken English for Effective Communication." *Souvenir of YMCA Toastmaster's Club of Hyderabad. Ninth Charter Night Anniversary,* 29 Apr.

605. ————. 1976
"Indian English." *Souvenir of the Sixth All-India Conference of Dravidian Linguistics, Andhra University, Waltair.* pp. 55-57.

606. ————. 1976
"Initial Consonant Clusters in English and Hindi." *CIEFL Newsletter.* 21. pp. 15-20.

607. ————. 1976
The Intelligibility of Indian English. Hyderabad, Central Institute of English and Foreign Languages. (Monograph No. 4. Shorter version of the book published in 1969.)

608. ————. 1970-71
"A Phonetic Analysis of English Spoken by a Group of Well-Educated Speakers From Uttar Pradesh." *Bulletin, Central Institute of English.* 8. pp. 1-9.

609. BANSAL, Ram Krishna and HARRISON, J.B. 1972
Spoken English for India : A Manual of Speech and Phonetics. Bombay, Orient Longman.

610. BANSAL, Ram Krishna. 1975
"Phonetics and the Study of Literature." *Bulletin, Central Institute of English and Foreign Languages.* 11. pp. 15-20.

611. ————. 1978
"Phonetic Research Relevant to English Language Teaching in India." Paper presented at the Workshop on Listening and Speaking held at SEAMEO RELC 13th Regional Seminar, Singapore, Apr. (Mimeographed..)

612. ————. 1978
The Phonology of Indian English, *IN* MOHAN, Ramesh. (ed) : *Indian Writing in English.* Madras, Orient Longman. pp. 101-114.

613. ————. 1979
"Spoken English in India : A Plea For Better Standards." *The Journal of English Studies* (Regional Engineering College, Warangal). 11 : 1. pp. 689-696.

614. ————. 1979
"Spoken English in India : A Phonological Study of Languages in Contact." *Wissenschaftliche Zeitschrift.* 28 : 5. pp. 679-684.

615. ————. 1979
"Vowel Duration in Hindi and English." *CIEFL Newsletter.* 15 : 4. pp. 7-9.

616. ————. 1981
"English and Hindi : A Contrastive Phonological Study." *CIEFL Bulletin.* 17 : 2. pp. 51-60.

617. ————. 1984
"Suprasegmental Features and the Teaching of Second Languages in India", *IN* RAJAPUROHIT, B.B. (ed) : *Papers in Phonetics and Phonology.* Manasagangotri, Mysore, Central Institute of Indian Languages. pp. 17-30.

618. BARRON, A.W.J. 1961
"The English Dental Fricatives in India." *Bulletin, Central Institute of English.* 1. pp. 84-86.

619. ————. 1961
"English Vowels for Indian Learners." *Bulletin, Central Institute of English.* 1. pp. 77-83.

620. ————. 1963
"English Consonants for Indian Learners." *Bulletin, Central Institute of English.* 3. pp. 96-104.

621. BEZ BORUAH, Direndranath.
A Comparative Study of the Phonologies of Assamese, Bengali and Oriya With Some Reference to the Problems of English Pronunciation. Thesis (Ph.D.)—University of Mysore, Mysore.

622. BHARATI, Surabhi. 1983
A Study of the Intonation Patterns in English Spoken by B.A. First Year Students of Vikram University. Thesis (M.Litt.)—Central Institute of English and Foreign Languages.

623. BHATIA, Kailash Chandra. 1957
"Angrezii 'R' Aur Hindi Me Uske Vibhinn Svarup.

(The English 'R' and Its Various Forms in Hindi.)" *Bharatiya Sahitya.* 2 : 4. pp. 81-88.

624. BONAR, A.G. 1968
"The Importance of Stress." *ELTI Bulletin.* 5. pp. 10-14.

625. BUSH, Clara N. 1967
"Some Acoustic Parameters of Speech and Their Relationships to the Perception of Dialect Differences." *TFSOL Quarterly.* 1 : 3. pp. 20-30. (About Indian, American and British English.)

626. ————. 1972
Temporal Ratios of Sound : Segments and the Perception of English Dialect Differences. The Hague, Mouton. (For Indian English, see pp. 666-672.)

627. CAMA, K.M. 1939
"A Study of the Native Hindustani Melody Pattern and the Acquired English Pattern With Special Reference to the Teaching of English in India." *Archives Ne'evlandaises Phonetique Experimental.* 11. pp. 103-110.

628. CANDLIN, Christopher. 1969
"Pronunciation Problems of Asian Immigrants." *English for Immigrants.* 2 : 2. pp. 23-29.

629. CHANA, Urmi and ROMAINE, Suzanne. 1984
"Evaluative Reactions to Punjabi/English Code-Switching." *Journal of Multilingual and Multicultural Development.* 5 : 6. pp. 447-473.

630. CHASWAL, Krishna Kumari. 1973
A Comparative Study of English and Hindi Intonation. Thesis (Research Diploma)—Central Institute of English and Foreign Languages, Hyderabad.

631. CHATURVEDI, M.G. 1973
A Contrastive Study of Hindi-English Phonology. Delhi. National.

632. ————. 1963
A Contrastive Study of Hindi-English Phonology. Hyderabad, Central Institute of English. (Unpublished research paper.)

633. CHAUDHARY, Shreesh C. 1979
A Remedial Course in English Fricatives for Maithili Speakers. Thesis (Diploma)—Central Institute of English and Foreign Languages, Hyderabad.

634. ————. 1984
Some Aspects of the Phonology of Indian English. Thesis (Ph.D.)—Central Institute of English and Foreign Languages, Hyderabad.

635. ————. 1984
"Some Low-Level Phenomenon in the Phonology of Indian English." *CIEFL Working Papers in Linguistics.* 1 : 1.

636. —————. 1985
Survey of English : South Kanara District : A Report, by Shreesh C. Chaudhary. Edited by K.C. Nambiar, Jacob Tharu and Radhakrishna Pillai. Hyderabad, Central Institute of English and Foreign Languages.

637. ————. 1986
"Teaching of Spoken English in India : Review and Suggestions." *Focus on English.* 2 : 2. pp. 13-21.

638. DAS, Rajendra Kishan. 1961
"Pronunciation Difficulties of Oriya Speakers Learning English." *Teaching English.* 6 : 4. pp. 35-43.

639. DATTA, Sunanda. 1972-73
"The Pronunciation of English by Bengali Speakers." *CIEFL Bulletin.* 9. pp. 35-40.

640. —————. 1975
"Towards an Effective Learning Programme for Bengali

Learners of English : Pronunciation." *CIEFL Bulletin.* 11. pp. 21-37.

641. DAVE, P.B. 1964
Excerpts From Writings Dealing With Indian Pronunciation. Thesis (Research Diploma)—Central Institute of English and Foreign Languages, Hyderabad.

642. ————. 1965
Indian English : A Study of the Pronunciation of English in Certain Regions of India. Thesis (Research Diploma)—Central Institute of English, Hyderabad.

643. DHALL, G.B. 1965
"Observation on Some Common Peculiarities in the English Speech of the People of Orissa." *Indian Linguistics.* 16. pp. 276-282.

644. DHAMIJA, Pushya Vibhooti 1976
A Phonological Description of Rajasthani English. Thesis (M.Litt.)—Central Institute of English and Foreign Languages. (Unpublished.)

645. ————. 1978
A Phonological Study of Rajasthani English. Thesis (Ph.D.)—Rajasthan University, Jaipur.

646. ————. 1980
Types of Nuclear Tone in English Spoken in Rajasthan." *Language Forum.* 6 : 1-2. pp. 24-30.

647. DHAR, Prabhas Chandra, 1977
The Segmental Phonemes of Tripura Bengali and Standard Indian English : A Contrastive Study With Pedagogical Implications. Thesis (M.Litt.)—Central Institute of English and Foreign Languages, Hyderabad.

648. DIXIT, Rajendra. 1976
"The Pronunciation of English in Indian Schools." *ELT Forum News.* 1 : 1. pp. 5-6.

649. DRY, D.P.L. 1971
"The Use of the Devanagari Script as a Phonemic Notation for the Teaching of English Pronunciation in Northern India", *IN* PERREN, G.E. and TRIM, J.L.M. (ed) : *Applications of Linguistics.* Cambridge, Cambridge University Press. pp. 189-192.

650. DUSTOOR, Phiroze Edulji. 1955
The Problem of Pronunciation. Agra. (Agra University Extension Lectures. 16-27.)

651. GARG, Ramesh C. 1969
A Description of Oriya English Segmental Phonemes. Thesis (M.Litt.)—University of Delhi, Delhi.

652. ————. 1980
A Study of Perception of English Speech Sounds by Mono and Bilingual Speakers of Hindi. Thesis (Ph.D.)—University of Delhi, Delhi. (Unpublished.)

653. GIRIJA NIRMALA, N. 1983
A Comparative Study of English Spoken by Teachers of English and Teachers of Other Subjects : A Study at the Undergraduate Level of the Nagarjuna University, Andhra Pradesh. Thesis (M.Litt.)—Central Institute of English and Foreign Languages, Hyderabad.

654. ————. 1985
A Comparative Study of English Spoken by Teachers of English and Teachers of Other Subjects and the Phonetic Correlates of 'Good' and 'Bad' Spoken English. Thesis (Ph.D.)—Central Institute of English and Foreign Languages, Hyderabad.

655. GOKHALE, Shridhar B. 1978
A Study of Intonation Patterns in Marathi and Marathi English. Thesis (M.Litt.)—Central Institute of English and Foreign Languages, Hyderabad.

656. ————. 1984
Prosodic Systems in Marathi and Marathi English. Thesis

(Ph.D.)—Central Institute of English and Foreign Languages, Hyderabad.

657. GOPALAKRISHNAN, G.S. 1960
"Some Observations on the South Indian Pronunciation of English." *Teaching English* (Bombay). 6 : 2. pp. 62-67.

658. GUPTA, Krishan Lal. 1982
Dogri English : A Phonological Study. Thesis (M.Litt.)—Central Institute of English and Foreign Languages.

659. GUPTA, Sagar Mal. 1980
Stress in U.P. English and Rule Ordering. Thesis (Ph.D.)—East-West Centre, University of Hawaii, Honolulu.

660. ————. 1980
"Vowel Reduction in Uttar Pradesh English : An Instrumental Study." *CIEFL Bulletin*. 16 : 1. pp. 31-40.

661. ————. 1981-82
"Vowel Alternation in Uttar Pradesh English." *Journal of the School of Languages* (Jawaharlal Nehru University). 8 : 1-2. pp. 17-29.

662. ————.
"Word Stress in Uttar Pradesh English and Its Effect on Intelligibility to Speakers of American English." *The Journal of English Language Teaching*. 16 : 4. pp. 105-112.

663. HAFIZULLAH, R. 1959
A Phonetic Study of 200 English Loan Words in Hindustani. Edinburgh, School of Applied Linguistics, University of Edinburgh. (Unpublished paper.)

664. HAI, M.A. and BALL, W.J. 1961.
The Sound Structures of English and Bengali. Dacca, University of Dacca.

665. HARRY, Pramila. 1962
A Study of Spoken Gujarati in Its Relation to the Teaching of English to Gujarati Learners. Thesis—School of Applied Linguistics, University of Edinburgh. (Unpublished.)

666. HASHMI, A. 1963
A Comparative Study of Some Phonological Features of Urdu-English. Edinburgh, School of Applied Linguistics, University of Edinburgh. (Unpublished paper.)

667. HILL, Leslie A. 1959
"Pronunciation Difficulties of Hindi Speakers Learning English." *Teaching English* (Bombay). 6 : 1. Aug. pp. 23-25.

668. ————. 1959-60
"A Comparison Between Initial Clusters in English and Hindi," *Transactions of the Linguistic Circle of Delhi, New Delhi.* pp. 37-40.

669. HUGHES, P. 1949
"Spoken English in India." *The Fortnightly.* (NSV. 165). Jan./Jun. pp. 39-43.

670. IRULAPPAN, K.M. 1978
A sociolinguistic Approach to the Realisation of English Consonants in Tamilian Speech, *IN Seminar on Phonology.* Annamalainagar, Advanced Centre for Dravidian Linguistics, Annamalai University.

671. ISMAEL, Sadikha, 1975
A Phonological Analysis of English Spoken by I Year University Students in Pondicherry. Thesis (M.Litt.)—Central Institute of English and Foreign Languages, Hyderabad. (Unpublished.)

672. JACKSON, Howard. 1981
"Pronunciation of English Consonants by Indian Learners." *ELT Journal.* 35. pp. 418-419.

673. JINDAL, Dharam Vir. 1985
Problems of Pronunciation of Individual Words of English as Spoken by the Teachers of English in the Rural Schools of Punjab. Thesis (Ph.D.)—Punjab University, Chandigarh. (Unpublished.)

674. JOSEPH, Komali. 1984
Intonation Patterns of Telugu-English. Thesis (M.Litt.)—Central Institute of English and Foreign Languages, Hyderabad.

675. JULKA, Satya Pal. 1970
The Role of Phonology in the Teaching of English Pronunciation to Punjabi-Speaking Students. Thesis (Diploma)—Institute of Science and Technology, University of Wales, Bongov.

676. KHCHRU, Braj B. 1959
An Instrumental Phonetic Analysis of Some Prosodic Features of Indian English and Received Pronunciation. Thesis (Diploma)—University of Edinburgh, Edinburgh.

677. KANUM, B.A. 1964-65
A Comparative Study of the Sound Structures of English and Bengali. Thesis—University of Leeds.

678. KELKAR, Ashok R. 1958
" 'Marathi English' : A Study in Foreign Accent." *Word.* 13. pp. 268-282 and 14. 1958. pp. 435- .

679. KHUBCHANDANI, Lachman Mulchand. 1966
"Bilingual Interference in Language Learning (Indian Pronunciation of English)." Paper presented at Seminar on Language Teaching, American Institute of Indian Studies, Poona.

680. KOHLI, A.L. 1971
"A Phonetician's Views on Indian English." *Awaz-i-Ustad.* 16 Sep.

681. KRISHNAMURTI, Bh. 1978
"Spelling Pronunciation in Indian English', *IN* MOHAN, Ramesh. (ed) : *Indian Writing in English.* Madras, Orient Longman. pp. 129-139

682. KRISHNAMURTHY, R. 1976-77.
The Tamilian Pronunciation of English. Annamalainagar, Annamalai University. (M.A. Paper.)

683. KYANI, S. 1964-65
Phonetics of Punjabi, With Notes on Teaching English Pronunciation to Punjabi Students. Thesis (Diploma)—University of Leeds.

684. LAHIRI, K.C. 1956
"Peculiarities in Spoken English of Indians and the Question of a Standard for Them." *Research Bulletin (Arts) of the Punjab University, Chandigarh.* 19 : 3. pp. 1-17.

685. LATHA, P. 1978
Intonation of Malayalam and Malayalee English : A Study in Comparison and Contrast. Thesis (M.Litt.)—Central Institute of English and Foreign Languages, Hyderabad.

686. LEE, IK-MO. 1971
A Study of Laryngeal Source Variables, Their Employment as Distinctive Cues for the Plosive Consonants of English, Hindi and Korean, and Their Inherent Distinguishability as Measured in a Non-Linguistic Perception Test. Thesis (Ph.D.)—Georgetown University.

687. LIMAYE, Mohan R. 1965
" 'H' for a Marathi Speaker of English. (The Problem of Aspiration.)" *ELT Journal.* 20 : 1. pp. 72-75.

688. LOVELL, Charles S. 1966
Evaluational Reactions of a Sample of College Students

From India to Spoken English and Hindi. Thesis (Ph.D.) —Kansas State University.

689. MASICA, C.P. ; KRISHNASWAMI, N. and CHATURVEDI, M.G. 1963
"A Comparison of the Sounds of Hindi and Tamil With the Sounds of English." *Bulletin, Central Institute of English*. 3. pp. 53-95.

690. MASICA, C.P. 1970
"Review of 'BANSAL, R.K. ; *The Intelligibility of Indian English : Measurement of the Intelligibility of Connected Speech and Sentence and Word Material Presented to Listeners of Different Nationalities.*' " *Language*, 46 : 3. pp. 730-735.

691. MASICA, C.P. and DAVE, P.B. 1972
The Sound System of Indian English. Hyderabad, Central Institute of English and Foreign Languages. (CIEFL Monograph No. 7.)

692. MATHUR, P.S. 1970
Word Accent in Indian English : Thesis (Diploma)—Central Institute of English and Foreign Languages, Hyderabad.

693. MOHAN, Kamal. 1964
"The English ; / as Replaced by Vowel Sounds in the English Speech of Indians." *Teaching English.* 8 : 2. pp. 7-11.

694. ————. 1964.
"An Investigation Into the Reading Aloud Habits of a Representative Group of Highly Educated Indians." *Teaching English.* 8 : 2. pp. 11-20.

695. ————. 1966
"A Note on 'a', 'an', 'the' and 'to' in RP and Spoken Indian English." *Teaching English.* 9 : 1. pp. 16-19.

696. ————. 1976
"A Note on /r/,/h/,/t/ and /I/ in RP and Indian Spoken English." *Teaching English.* 9 : 2.

697. —————. 1970
Spoken English in Hindi Speaking Area : A Phonetic and Morphological Study. Thesis (Ph.D.)—Ravishankar University.

698. MULGUND, V.V. 1974
Some Problems of the Kannada Speakers of Dharwar Region, Karnataka State in the Pronunciation of English and a Few Suggested Remedial Drills. Thesis (Research Diploma)—Central Institute of English and Forcign Languages, Hyderabad.

699. MURTHY, Suman. 1981
A Study of the Attitudinal Function of Intonation in Kannada English. Thesis (M.Litt.)—Central Institute of English and Foreign Languages, Hyderabad.

700. NADKARNI, M.V. 1964-65
"Teaching Spoken English in Colleges." *Bulletin of the Central Institute of English.* 4 and 5. pp. 94-113.

701. NAGARAJAN, Hemlatha. 1985
Some Phonetic Featurcs of Tamilian English. Thesis (M.Litt.)—Central Institute of English and Foreign Languages, Hyderabad.

702. NAGESWARA RAO, E. 1983
The English Pronunciation of Telugu Speakers, *IN* NAGESWARA RAO, E. : *Teaching a Second Language and Other Essays.* Hyderabad, Pushyami. pp. 26-41.

703. NAGESWARA RAO, E. 1983
"Some Problems in the English Pronunciation of Telugu Speakers." *CIEFL Newsletter*: 28 : 3-4. pp. 11-14.

704. NASIRUDDIN KHAN. 1974
A Phonological Analysis of English Spoken by All India Radio Newsreaders. Thesis (Research Diploma)—Central Institute of English and Foreign Languages, Hyderabad.

705. NIHALANI, Paroo K. 1286
"Received British Pronunciation and the Teaching of English in Commonwealth Countries." Paper presented at the 4th International Conference on the Teaching of English held at Carleton University, Ottawa, Canada, 11-16 May.

706. PANDEY, G.S. 1984
A Phonological Study of English Spoken by the Educated Assamese. Thesis (M.Litt.)—Central Institute of English and Foreign Languages.

707. PANDEY, Pramod Kumar. 1980
Word Stress in Hindustani English : A Generative Phonological Study. Thesis (M.Litt.)—Central Institute of English and Foreign Languages, Hyderabad. (Unpublished.)

708. ————. 1981
"On a Description of the Phonology of Indian English." *CIEFL Bulletin.* 17 : 1. pp. 11-19.

709. ————. 1985
Word Accentuation in Hindustani English in Relation to Word Accents in English and Hindi. Thesis (Ph.D.)—University of Poona, Poona.

710. PANDIT, Prabodh B. 1964
"Indian Re-adjustments in the English Consonant System." *Indian Linguistics.* 25. pp. 202-205.

711. PANT, H.C. 1967
A Manual of Spoken English for India. Thesis (Research

Diploma)—Central Institute of English and Foreign Languages, Hyderabad.

712. PATEL, M.S. 1959
The Representation of English Sounds in the Gujarati Script. Baroda, University of Baroda.

713. PATEL, S.M. 1977
Phonology of Indian Loan Words in English. Thesis (Ph.D.)—Marathwada University, Marathwada.

714. PATHAK, R.S. 1972
"The Teaching of English Pronunciation Through a Devanagari Phoneme Notation." *ELTI Bulletin.* 10. pp. 31-41. (Also in : *Bulletin, Central Institute of English and Foreign Languages*, 10. 1974.

715. PATIL, Chandrasekhar. 1975
A Contrastive Study of Intonation Patterns in Kannada and English. Thesis (Ph.D.)—Karnataka University.

716. PAUL, Probodh Chandra. 1972
A Contrastive Study of Sound Structures of English and Bengali for Facilitating English Pronunciation Learning by the Bengalis. Thesis (Ph.D.)—University of Calcutta, Calcutta.

717. ————. 1977
"The Question of Our Speeeh. (A Note on English Pronunciation.)" *Teacher Today.* 20 : 2. pp. 6-12.

718. PITCHAI, J. Anthony. 1983
Word Accent in Tamilian English Spoken by the Undergraduate Students of the Sethupathy Government College, Ramnad. Thesis (M. Litt.)– Central Institute of English and Foreign Languages, Hyderabad.

719. ————.
Accent and Rhythm in Tamilian English. Thesis (Ph.D.)—

Central Institute of English and Foreign Languages, Hyderabad. (In progress.)

720. PLECHKO, Z.P. 1971
"Nekotorye Foneticheskie Osobennosti Angliiskogo Yazyka v Indii. (Some Phonetic Peculiarities of Indian English.)" *Inostrannye Yazyki v Vysshei Shkole* (Moskva.) 6.

721. PRABHAKAR BABU, B.A. 1970-71
"Prosodic Features in Indian English : Stress, Rhythm and Intonation." *Bulletin, Central Institute of English.* 8. pp. 33-39.

722. ————. 1971
Prosodic Features in Indian English : Stress, Rhythm and Intonation. Thesis (Research Diploma)—Central Institute of English and Foreign Languages, Hyderabad.

723. ————. 1975
A Phonetic and Phonological Study of Some Characteristic Features of Telugu English Including Reference to the Source and Target Languages. Thesis (M.Phil.)—University of London, London.

724. ————. 1977
A Phonological Study of English Spoken by Telugu Speakers in Andhara Pradesh. Thesis (Ph.D.)—Osmania University, Hyderabad.

725. PRASAD, Gorakh. 1957
"Devanaagarii me Angrezii Shabdokaa Uchaaran. (Pronunciation of English Words in Devanagari.)" *Nagari Pracharini Patrika.* 62. pp. 311-312.

726. PRASAD, Nalini. 1983
Intonation of Tamil English—A Study at the Discourse Level. Thesis (M.Litt.)—Central Institute of English and Foreign Languages, Hyderabad.

727. PREMALATA, M. 1978
The Vowels of Malayalee English: Generative Phonological Study. Thesis (M.Litt.)—Central Institute of English and Foreign Languages, Hyderabad.

728. RAHMAN, Khaliqur. 1982
Sound-Segments and Word Stress in English Spoken by a Group of Speakers at Raipur, Madhya Pradesh. Thesis (M.Litt.)—Central Institute of English and Foreign Languages, Hyderabad.

729. ————. 1985
"Word-Stress in Indian English With Special Reference to English Spoken at Raipur, Madhya Pradesh." Paper presented at the National Seminar on Indian English, 15-16 Mar., Department of Linguistics, University of Delhi.

730. ————. 1986
Stress Factors in Indian English and British English, *IN* RAJAPUROHIT, B.B. (ed): *Papers in Phonetics and Phonology*. Vol. 2. Mysore, Central Institute of Indian Languages. (Forthcoming.)

731. ————.
Description of English Spoken by 20 Educated People at Raipur, Madhya Pradesh: A Phonetic and Phonological Study. Thesis (Ph.D.)—Central Institute of English and Foreign Languages, Hyderabad. (In progress.)

732. RAMUNNI, Kavita. 1976
Subjective Reactions to Regional and Non-Regional English Accents in India. Thesis (M.Litt.)—Central Institute of English and Foreign Languages, Hyderabad.

733. RATHORE, R.S. 1970
"Teaching of English Pronunciation in the Schools of Gujarat and a Comparison of English and Gujarati Phonemes." *Educational Forum*. 15 : 1. pp. 7-17.

734. RAZDAN, Giridhari Lal. 1970
A Description of Kashmiri English Segmental Phonemes. Thesis (M.A.)—University of Delhi, Delhi.

735. REGU, K. 1975
Phonic Interference Between Malayalam and English, *IN* RADHAKRISHNAN, R. (eds) : *Research and Criticism.* Annamalainagar, Annamalai University. pp. 122-127.

736. ROY, Mira. 1969
"Some Problems of English Consonants for a Bengali Speaker of English." *English Language Teaching Journal.* 23 : 3. pp. 268-270.

737. ————. 1975
"Bengali Difficulties With the Sounds of English." *English Language Teaching Journal.* 30 : 1.

738. RUBDY, Rani Sumant. 1975
A Phonological Analysis of English Spoken by Ten Marathi Speakers From Maharashtra. Thesis (M.Litt.)—Central Institute of English and Foreign Languages, Hyderabad.

739. SADANAND, Kamlesh. 1973
A Course in Spoken English For Use in India. Thesis (Research Diploma)—Central Institute of English and Foreign Languages, Hyderabad.

740. SADANAND, Suchitra. 1981
Stress in Malayalee English : A Generative Phonological Approach. Thesis (M.Litt.)- Central Institute of English and Foreign Languages, Hyderabad.

741. ————. 1985
"The Phonology of Malayali English." Paper presented at the National Seminar on Indian English, Department of Linguistics, University of Delhi, 15-16 Mar.

742. SAHGAL, Anju and AGNIHOTRI, Ramakant. 1985
"Is Indian English Retroflexed and r-Full ?" Paper presented at the National Seminar on Indian English, Department of Linguistics, University of Delhi, 15-16 Mar.

743. SAILAJA, P. 1985
Some Aspects of the Vowel Phonology of Telugu and Telugu English. Thesis (M. Litt.)—Central Institute of English and Foreign Languages, Hyderabad.

744. SAYYID, M.A.W. 1966
"English Consonants Difficult for Urdu Learners." *Philippine Journal for Language Teaching.* 4 : 1-2. pp. 29-33.

745. SEETHA, R. 1982
The System of Vowels In the English Spoken by the Undergraduate Students of Pondicherry : An Articulatory and Acoustic Study. Thesis (M.Litt.)—Central Institute of English and Foreign Languages, Hyderabad.

746. ————. 1986.
Spoken Indian English. Thesis (Ph.D.)—Central Institute of English and Foreign Languages, Hyderabad. (In progress.)

747. SESHADRI, C.K. 1970
"TESL and Spoken English in the Indian Context." *Journal, M.S. University of Baroda.* 19 : 1. pp. 1-6.

748. SETHI, Jitendra. 1971
Intonation of Statements and Questions in Punjabi. Hyderabad, Central Institute of English. (Monograph No. 6.)

749. ————. 1976
English Spoken by Educated Punjabi Speakers in India : A Phonological Study. Thesis (Ph D.)—Punjab University, Chandigarh. (Unpublished.)

750. ————. 1979
"Consonant System in Educated Punjabi-Speakers' English." *CIEFL Bulletin.* 15 : 2. pp. 21-36.

751. ————. 1980
"Consonant Clusters in Educated Punjabi-Speakers' English." *CIEFL Bulletin.* 16 : 1. pp. 7-29 16 : 2. 1980. pp. 31-55 and 17 : 2. 1980. pp. 61-71.

752. ————. 1980
"The Vowel System in Educated Punjabi-Speakers' English." *Journal of the International Phonetic Association.* 10. 1980. pp. 64-73. (First appeared in *CIEFL Bulletin.* 14 : 2. 1978. pp. 35-48.)

753. ————. 1981
"Phonological Study of Educated Panjabi Speakers." Paper presented at the 16th Regional Seminar, SEAMEO Regional Language Centre, Singapore.

754. SHUKLA, S.P. 1970
A Phonological Analysis of English Spoken by a Group of Educated People With Hindi as Their Mother Tongue. Hyderabad, Central Institute of English. (Term paper.)

755. SINGH, N. 1966-67.
A Phonetic Study of Punjabi Segmental Phonemes and Their Comparison With English. Thesis—University of Wales. (Unpublished.)

756. SINGH, Sadanand and BLACK, J.W. 1966
"Study of Twenty-Six Intervocalic Consonants as Spoken and Recognised by Four Language Groups." *Journal of the Acoustic Society of America.* 39. pp. 372-387.

757. SINGH, Sadanand. 1967
Initially and Transitionally Truncated Pre-Vocalic English Consonants Spoken and Recognised by Native Hindi and English Speakers, *IN Tenth International Conference of Linguists, Bucharest. 1967.* Vol. 4. pp. 245-255.

758. SISSON, Ralph Richard. 1968
A Comparative Analysis of the Speech Sound Systems of Southern British English and Hindi. Thesis (Ph.D.)—New York University, New York.

759. ————. 1971
"The Description and Comparison of Stress in Southern British English and Hindi." *Linguistics.* 17. pp. 35-60.

760. SMITH, G.P. 1975
"Some Difficulties of Telugu Students of English." *Bulletin, Central Institute of English and Foreign Languages.* 11. pp. 57-72

761. SOHN, Johny Y. 1961
"Teaching English Sounds to Tamil Speaking Students." *U.S. Army Language School Review.* 16. Spring. pp. 16-32.

762. SOOD, S.C. 1978
"A Plea For Spoken English." *CIEFL Newsletter.* 14 : 2-3. pp. 24-26.

763. SPENCER, John W. 1957
"Notes on the Pronunciation Problem." *Shiksha : The Jonrnal of the Education Department*, U.P. 9 : 4. Apr. pp. 91-97.

764. SREEKANTAIYA, T.N. 1940
"English as the Kannadigas Speak It." *Bulletin of Phonetic Studies* (Mysore University Phonetic Association). 1. pp. 11-19.

765. SRIVASTAVA, Indra Swarup. 1967
"English Pronunciation of Hindi Speaking Pupils." *Educational Review.* 73 : 8. pp. 177-179.

766. ————. 1968
"Some Pronunciation Problems in English for Hindi-Speaking Pupils." *Bulletin of the English Language Teaching Institute, Allahabad.* 4. pp. 26-28.

767. SUBRAMANIAM, A. 1964
Phonological Study of Tamilian English. Thesis (M.A.)—Annamalai University, Annamalainagar.

768. SURYANARAYANA RAO, Kolar. 1961
"A Footnote to the Indian Pronunciation of the Initial /P/, /T/, /K/, /V/and /W/ in English." *Indian Linguistics.* 22. pp. 160-163.

769. SUSEENDIRARAJAH, S. 1972
"Some Pronunciation Problems of Tamil Speakers Learning English." *Indian Linguistics*. 33 : 1. pp. 59-66.

770. TAYLOR, Susan. 1967
A Preliminary Study of the Stress System in Indian English. Urbana, Ill., University of Illinois (Unpublished paper.)

771. ————. 1975
A Preliminary Study of Stress and Intonation in the English of Hindi and American Speakers. Urbana, Division of English as a Second Language, University of Illinois. (Unpublished paper.)

772. THEODORE, B. 1966
Better English Pronunciation of Commonly Mispronunced Words (*English-Telugu*). Narsapur, Sitaram Press.

773. THYAGARAJU, A.F. 1930
"On the Pronunciation of English by South Indians." *Quarterly Journal of the Mythic Society*. pp. 311-313.

774. TICKOO, M.L. 1963
"English Pronunciation in India : The Choice of a Model." *Language Learning*. 13 : 3, pp. 171-175.

775. UPENDRAN, S.
The Intelligibility of English Spoken by Tamilians. Thesis (M.Litt.)—Central Institute of English and Foreign Languages, Hyderabad.

776. ————. 1985
"Acquisition of Stress in Bisyllabic Words." Paper presented at the National Seminar on Indian English, 15-16 Mar., Department of Linguistics, University of Delhi.

777. VALENTINE, Elias. 1969
The Phonology of Anglo-Indian English. Thesis (Ph.D.)—University of Kerala. (Unpublished.)

778. ————. 1978
Some Non-Segmental Features of Anglo-Indian English, *IN* MANUEL, M. and AYYAPPA PANIKER, K. (eds) : *English and India.* Madras, Macmillan. pp. 190-212.

779. VARMA, Ravi S. 1972
"A Note on Phonologic Substitution in English Loan Words in Hindi." *Indian Linguistics.* 33 : 2. pp. 169-173.

780. VARMA, Siddheswar. 1957
"The Pronunciation of English in North Western India." *Indian Linguistics.* 18. pp. 86-88.

781. VELAYUDHAN ASARI, S. 1970
Contrastive Phonology of English and Malayalam. Thesis (Ph.D.)—Kerala University.

782. VELAYUDHAN, S. 1984
"Frequency of Speech Sounds of English and Malayalam." *RIE Journal.* 1 : 1. pp. 43-53.

783. VIJAYAKRISHNAN, K.G. 1978
Stress in Tamil English. Thesis (M.Litt.)—Central Isntitute of English and Foreign Languages, Hyderabad. (Unpublished.)

784. VISWANATH, L. 1962
Sounds of English for Urdu Speakers of Hyderabad : Record of Difficulties Encountered. Hyderabad, Central Institute of English. (Unpublished research report.)

785. ————. 1963-64
Kanarese and English : A Comparison of Their Phonologies. Bangov, University of North Wales. (Unpublished paper.)

786. VISWESWARA, C. 1972
"Teaching English Sounds to Indian Students—Consonants." *English in Gujarat.* 1 : 2. pp. 16-18.

787. ————. 1972
"Teaching English Sounds to Indian Students—Diphthongs." *English in Gujarat.* 1 : 1. pp. 6-9.

788. VORA, I.A. 1975
"Contrastive Analysis of English and Gujarati Consonants." *Journal of Educational Psychology.* 32 : 4. pp. 226-247.

789. WELLS, J.C. 1982
Accents of English. 3 Vol. London, Cambridge University Press. (See Chapter 9 : 1 of volume 3 for Indian English. pp. 623-632.)

790. WILLIAMS, T. Edward. 1972
A Comparative Note on the Stop Phonemes in Tamil and English, *IN* ALL INDIA University Tamil Teachers' Association. : *Collection of Papers Presented in the Fourth Conference—Seminar.* Annamalainagar, A.I.U. T.T.A. pp. 326-330.

791. WILSON, R.M. 1969-70
Aspects of Accent and Intonation in English and Hindi. Cardiff, Institute of Science and Technology, University of Wales.

792. YARDI, V.V.
A Comparison of the Sounds of Marathi and English. Thesis (Research Diploma)—Central Institute of English and Foreign Languages, Hyderabad.

793. ————. 1977-78
"Teaching English Pure Vowels to the Marathi Learner : Some Suggestions." *ELT Journal.* 32. pp. 303-307.

794. ————. 1984
A Note on Word Accent in Marathi and English, *IN* AMUR, G.S., *et al.* (eds) : *Essays on Comparative Literature and Linguistics.* New Delhi, Sterling pp. 159-162.

8. GRAMMATICAL ASPECTS

795. AGNIHOTRI, Rama Kant ; KHANNA, A.L. and MUKHERJEE, Aditi. 1984
"The Use of Articles in Indian English : Errors and Pedagogical Implications." *IRAL*. 22 : 2. pp. 115-129.

796. ————. 1986
Variations in the Use of Tenses in English : A Sociolinguistic Perspective. (A Report), *IN* BAHRI, U.S. (ed) : *Papers in Language and Linguistics*. New Delhi, Bahri. pp. 96-116.

797. AITCHISON, Jean and AGNIHOTRI, Rama Kant, 1985
"I Deny That I'm Incapable of Working All Night." : Divergence of Negative Structures in British and Indian English, *IN* EATON, Roger, *et al* (ed) : *Papers From the 4th International Conference on English Historical Linguistics, Amsterdam, 10-13 Apr.* Amsterdam, John Benjamins. pp. 3-14.

798. ALAM, Qaiser Zoha. 1980
"Commands and Requests in English and Urdu." *Indian Linguistics*. 41 ; 3-4. pp. 129-132.

799. AULAKH, Gurinder ; GUMPERZ, John J. and KALTMAN, Hannah. 1978.
Thematic Structure and Progression in Indian English Discourse. Berkeley, University of California. Manuscrip.

800. BENDIX, Edward K. 1965
Componential Analysis of General Vocabulary—The Semantic Structure of a Set of Verbs in English, Hindi and Japanese. Thesis (Ph. D.)—Columbia University.

801. BHARGAVA, Prem Sagar. 1968
Linguistic Interference From Hindi, Urdu and Punjabi and Internal Analogy in the Grammar of Indian English. Thesis (Ph. D.)—Cornell University.

802. BHATIA, Aban Tavadia. 1973
An Analysis of Deviant Language Behaviour in English Composition of Undergraduate Students at the University of Delhi and Its Implications for Teaching. Thesis (Ph.D.) —University of Texas, Austin.

803. BHATIA, Kailash Chandra. 1963
"Hindi Me Angrezi Aagat Shabdo Kaa Ling. (The Gender of English Loan-Words in Hindi.)" *Bhasha.* 2 : 4. pp. 56-60.

804. BROWNING, Dorothy Anne. 1967
Constructive Collocational Analysis With Examples From Hindi and English. Thesis (Ph. D.)-- University of Texas, Texas.

805. CHIBBER, S.D.S. 1973
Interference in the Time-Base of Indian English. Thesis (M. A.)—University of Manchester, Manchester.

806. DANIEL, James R. 1981
The Intensifier 'Very'—'Mika' in English and Tamil, *IN* A.I.U.T.T.A. : *Collection of Papers Presented in the 14th Conference - Seminar.* Annamalainagar, A.I.U.T.T.A. pp. 187-192.

807. ——. 1982
The Focusing Adverb 'Only-Muttum' in English and Tamil, *IN* A.I.U.T.T.A. : *Collection of Papers presented in the 14th Conference-Seminar.* Annamalainagar, A.I.U. T.T.A. pp. 187-192.

808. ——. 1983
Formulaic Adverbials in English and Tamil, *IN* A.I.U. T.T.A. : *Collection of Papers Presented in the 13th Con-*

ference-Seminar. Annamalainagar, A.I.U.T.T.A. pp. 182-186.

809. DESHPANDE, A.S. and BIMAYE, K.V. 1986
"Objective Tests of English Prove Better Than Essay Type Examination to Assess Writing Ability in English". *IN* INDIA. MINISTRY OF PERSONNEL, PUBLIC GRIEVANCES AND PENSIONS. STAFF SELECTION COMMISSION. : Monograph on Testing Proficiency in Englishes Language. New Delhi, the Ministry. pp. 64-76.

810. DHONGDE, Ashwini. 1987
"The Language of Advertising." *Language Forum*. 13. pp. 211-220.

811. DHONGDE, Ramesh Vaman.
Tense, Aspect and Mood in English and Marathi. Thesis (Ph. D.)—Poona University, Poona.

812. DOLKE, A.M. 1986
Effectiveness of Objective Type Tests of English Language in Personnel Selection, *IN* INDIA. MINISTRY OF PERSONNEL, PUBLIC GRIEVANCES AND PENSIONS. STAFF SELECTION COMMISSION. : *Monograph on Testing Proficiency in English Language* New Delhi, the Ministry. pp. 30-38.

813. DUSTOOR, Phiroze Edulji. 1946
"An Introduction to the Study of English Usage in India" *Longman' Miscellany*. 4. pp. 131-146.

814. ——. 1954
"Missing and Intrusice Article in Indian English." *Allahabad University Studies* 31. pp. 1-70.

815. ——. 1955.
"Wrong, Usurping and Dispossessed Article in Indian English." *Allahabad University Studies*. 32. pp. 1-17.

816. DWIVEDI, R.K. 1969
Grammatical and Lexical Analysis of Registers of English Used in India : Administrative. Thesis (Research Diploma)—Central Institute of English and Foreign Languages.

817. FOX, Robert Paul. 1968
A Transformational Treatment of Indian English Syntax. Thesis (Ph. D.) —University of Illinois, Urbana, Ill.

818. GUMPERZ, John J. ; AULAKH, Gurinder and KALTMAN, Hannah. 1982
Thematic Structure and Progression in Discourse, *IN* GUMPERZ, John J. (ed) : *Language and Social Identity.* Cambridge, Cambridge University Press. pp. 22-56.

819. HIRUDAYARAJ, A. 1986
A Contrastive Study of Relative Clause in English and Tamil with Reference to the Difficulties of Tamil Learners of English. Thesis (Ph. D.)– Madurai-Kamaraj University, Madurai. (In progress.)

820. INDIRA, Varanasi. 1980
"Imperatives and Emotive predicates in Telugu and English : A Study in Linguistic Analysis." *Indian Linguistics.* 41 : 3-4. pp. 161-169.

821. JAIN, Mahavir P. 1985
"English in India : Its Syntactic, Semantic and Pragmatic Characteristics." Paper presented at the National Seminar on Indian English, Department of Linguistics, University of of Delhi, 15-16 Mar.

822. JALIL, M.A. 1963
Major Difficulties Experienced by Bengali Learners of English With Regard to Grammar and Sentence Structure. Leeds, University of Leeds. (Unpublished paper.)

823. JAYARAMAN, R.K. 1978
A Syntactic ond Semantic Study of Some Aspects of Tense

and Time in Tamil and English. Thesis (M. Litt.)—Central Institute of English and Foreign Languages, Hyderabad.

824. KALTMANN, Hannah. 1978
Thematic Structure and Progressing in Indian English Discourse. (Unpublished draft.)

825. KAPOOR, Premlata. 1985
"Various Fossilized Structures in Indian English." Paper presented at the National Seminar on Indian English, Department of Linguistics, University of Delhi, 15-16 Mar.

826. KINDERSLEY, A.F. 1938
"Notes on the Indian Idiom of English : Style, Syntax and Vocabulary." *Transactions of the Philological Society*. (Oxford). pp. 25-34.

827. KULKARNI, D.N.
—S Genitives in Indian English. Thesis (Ph. D.) Shivaji University, Kolhapur. (In Progress.)

828. KURLA, Shree Prakash. 1969.
"Hindi Me Aagat Angrezi Shabdo Ki Ling Ayavasthaa, (Gender System of English Loan-Words Hindi.)" *Bhasha* 8 : 4. pp. 71-75.

829. KWIATEK, Peter J. 1985
"Just in Indian English." Paper presented at the National Seminar on Indian English, Department of Linguistics, University of Delhi, 15-16 Mar.

830. MAHAJAN, Gyaneam and MAHAJAN, Anoop Kumar. 1985
"Notes on the Syntax of Indian English." Paper presented at the National Seminar on Indian English, Department of Linguistics, University of Delhi, 15-16 Mar.

831. MISHRA, Arpita. 1980
Discovering Connection, *IN Proceedings of the 6th Annual Meeting of the Berkeley Linguistic Society, 16-18 Feb.* pp. 73-83. (Also in : *Language ond Social Identity*, ed. by John J. Gumperz. Cambridge, 1982. pp. 55-71).

832. MODY, Jagmohandas Jagjivandas. 1961-67
A Comparative Study of English and Gujarathi Syntaxes. Thesis (Ph. D.)—M.S. University, Baroda.

833. MOHAN, Kamal. 1962
English in India : Some Observations on Usage. Hyderabad, Central Institute of English. (Unpublished research report.)

834. MUTHURAMAN, K.R. 1975
A Contrastive Study of Post—Positions in Tamil and in English, *IN All India University Tamil Teachers' Association. : Collection of Papers Presented in the Seventh Conference—Seminar.* Nagercoil, S.T. Hindu College. pp. 593-598.

835. NIHALANI, Narsu K. 1969
An Analysis of Some Aspects of the Thematic Organization of the Clause in Contemporary Written Indian Journalistic English. Thesis (Diploma)—Central Institute of English and Foreign Languages, Hyderabad. (Unpublished.)

836. NIHALANI, Narsu K.
A Study of the Semantics and Collocability of Certain Verbs in Indian English. Thesis (Ph. D.)—Marathwada University, Aurangabad. (In progress.)

837. PANDEY, Pramode K, 1981
"The Underlying Structure of a Derived Dialect-Evidence From Hindustani English." *IJDL.* 10 : 1. pp. 100-121.

838. PANDYA, Indubala Hiren. 1962-75

A Study of the English Language Used in Indian Press Advertising. Thesis (Ph. D.)—South Gujarat University.

839. ———. 1976
"Deviations in Advertising English in India." *Indian Linguistics.* 37 : 2. pp. 102-114.

840. ———. 1977
English Language in Advertising : A Linguistic Study of Indian Press Advertising. Delhi, Ajanta.

841. ———. 1980
"Cataphoric Cohesion and Other Distinctive Features of Indian Advertising English." *Osmania Papers in Linguistics.* 6. pp. 41-52.

842. PANDYA, Indubala H. 1987
"Clause Structure of Advertising English." *Language Forum.* 13. pp. 193-209.

843. PARASHER, S.V. 1983.
"Indian English : Certaln Grammatical, Lexical and Stylistic Features." *English World-Wide : A Journal of Varieties of English.* 4 : 1. pp. 27-42.

844. PATIL, B.N. 1986
If Conditionals in Indian English. Thesis (M. Phil.) – Shivaji University, Kolhapur. (In progress.)

845. PATIL, KULKARNI, C.T.
Exploration Into the Use of Articles in Indian English. Thesis (Ph. D.) – Shivaji University, Kolhapur. (In Progress.)

846. PATNAIK, B.N. and GEETHA, K. 1985
"Semantics of Some Auxiliary Verbs in Indian English". Paper presented at the National Seminar on Indian English, Department of Linguistics, University of Delhi, 15-16 Mar.

847. PATTNAIK, Umesh Prasad. 1983
Oriya English and the Ross Constraints – A Study. Thesis (M. Litt.)–Central Institute of English and Foreign Languages, Hyderabad.

848. PERINPANAYAGAM, G.T.R. 1964
"Some Difficulties in the Teaching of English as a Second Language to Tamil Students." *Journal of the National Education Society of Ceylon.* 13 : 1. pp. 58-73.

849. RAMASWAMY, K. 1973
A Contrastive Analysis of Relative Clause in Tamil and English. Thesis (Ph. D.) —Annamalai University, Annamalainagar.

850. RAMTHIRTHKAR, Sheela. 1986
Some, Any, and Their Compounds in Indian English. Thesis (M. Phil.)–Shivaji University, Kolhapur.

851. RANGAN, K. 1973
A Contrastive Analysis of the Grammatical Structure of Tamil and English. Thesis (Ph. D.)—Delhi University, Delhi.

852. RUBDY, Rani Sumant. 1981
A Study of Some Written Varieties of Indian English. Thesis (Ph. D.) — Central Institute of English and Foreign Languages, Hyderabad.

853. SAH, Prajapati Prasad. 1971
A Generative Semantic Treatment of Some Aspects of English and Hindi Grammar. Thesis (Ph. D.)—University of York.

854. SAHGAL, Anju and AGNIHOTRI, Rama Kant. 1985
"Syntax–The Common Bond : Acceptability of Syntactic Deviances in Indian English." *English World-Wide.* 6 : 1. pp. 117-129.

855. SCUR, G.S. and EROCHINA, N. K. 1979
"Variativnost v Glagol'nyx Slovosocetanijax v Anglij-

skom Jazyke India. (Variation in verb Phrases in English of India.)" *Zeitschrift fur Phonetik, Sprachwissenschaft und Kommunikations—forchung.* 33. pp. 439-444.

856. SEKHON, Gurkirpal Singh
Contrastive Study of the Verb Phrase in Punjabi and English. Thesis (Ph. D.) —Punjabi University.

857. SHEOREY, Ravindra. 1971
The Language of Indian English Newspaper Reporting(An Analysis of Its Structure and Vocabulary). Thesis (Research Diploma)— Central Institute of English and Foreign Languages.

858. SHINDE, Jayaprakash A.
A Study of the Behaviour of a Set of Verbs in Indian English. Thesis (Ph. D.)—Shivaji University, Kolhapur. (In progress.)

859. SHINGATE, S.T. 1966
The Phrasal Verbs in Indian English With Particles 'Up' and 'Down'. Thesis (M. Phil.)—Shivaji University, Kolhapur. (In progress.)

860. SINGH, Rajendra. 1977
"A Note on Supra Syntactic Interference : Exemplified by the Hindi Speaking Advanced Students' Discourse Conventions of the Native Language of English." *ITL : Review of Applied Linguistics.* 37. pp. 92-96.

861. SINHA, Anil Chandra. 1970
Predicate Complement Constructions in Hindi and English Thesis (Ph. D.)—York University, York.

862. SINHA, Smita. 1985
"Absolutive Constructions in Indian English." Paper presented at the National Seminar on Indian English, Department of Linguistics, University of Delhi, 15-16 Mar.

863. SRIVASTAVA, Indra Swarup. 1970
"Word Order Problems for Hindi Students of English." *Educational Review.* 76 : 3. pp. 63-65.

864. SRIVASTAVA, R.N. and CHOPRA, S.K. 1983
"Abbreviations and Acronyms in Indian Setting." *International Journal of Dravidian Linguistics.* 12 : 2. pp. 345-365.

865. SUSEENDIRA RAJAH, S. 1968-69.
Contrastive Study of Ceylon Tamil and English, *IN Proceedings of the First International Conference Seminar of Tamil Studies Kuala Lumpur, 1966.* Kuala Lumpur, Department of Indian Studies, University of Malaya, Vol. 2. pp. 751-756.

866. SWAMINATHAN, R. 1967
"Contrastive Analysis...Indian English." *The Journal of English Language Teaching* (Madras). 3 : 2. pp. 55-59.

867. TAVADIA, Aban Maneckshaw. 1971
Erratic Behaviour of Nouns and Verbs in Indian English : A Study in Generative Semantics. Thesis (M. Litt.)—University nf Delhi.

868. THEIVANATHAM PILLAI, K.A. 1968
"Some Structural Differences Between English and Tamil and Their Implications for Teaching. Part 1." *English For Our Schools, Ceylon.* 1 : 3. pp. 7-9.

869. ——. 1970
"A Comparative Study of the English and Tamil Auxiliary Verb Systems and Prediction of Learning Problems for Tamil Students of English." *IRAL.* 8 : 1. pp. 21-47

870. VALENTINE, Elias. 1972
Nominal Inflections in Malayaly English *IN Proceedings of the First All India Conference of Dravidian Linguists 1971.* Kariavattam, Trivandrum, Dravidian Linguistics Association. pp. 550-555.

871. VASUDEVA, Harender Nath. 1971
A Constrastive Study of Tense, Mood and Aspect in

English and Hindi. Thesis (Ph. D.)—University of Michigan.

872. VERMA, Shivendra Kishore. 1964
A Study in Systematic Description of Hindi Grammar and Comparison of the Hindi and English Verbal Group. Thesis (Ph. D.)--University of Edinburgh. (Unpublished)

873. ——. 1973
"The Systemicness of Indian English." *ITL : Review of Applied Linguistics.* 22. pp. 1-9.

874. ——. 1978
Syntactic Irregularities in Indian English. *IN* MOHAN, Ramesh. (ed) : *Indian Writing in English.* Madras, Orient Longman. pp. 207-220.

875. ——. 1980
"Swadeshi English : Form and Function." *Indian Linguistics.* 41 : 2. pp. 73-84.

876. WILLIAMS, T. Edward. 1965
A Contrastive Analysis af Tamil and English. Thesis (Ph. D.) —Annamalai University, Annamalainagar.

---

9. ERRORS AND REMEDIES

---

877. AKRUWALA, C.K. 1972
"A Study of Common Errors in English by the Pupils of the Schools of Combay, Gujarat." *Progress of Education.* 47 : 4. pp. 136-142.

878. ALAM, Quiser Zoha. 1976
"English Spelling—The Problem of Indian Learners." *Indian Journal of Applied Linguistics.* 2 : 2. pp. 75-86.

879. BAKSI, D.R. 1978
A Linguistic Analysis of Errors in the Verbal Group in English Made by Punjabi Speaking Students. Thesis (M. Litt.)—Central Institute of English and Foreign Languages, Hyderabad,

880. BELL, Roger T. 1973
"The English of an Indian Immigrant : An Essay in Error Analysis." *ITL Review of Applied Linguistics*. 22. pp. 11-61.

881. BHALLA, Inderjit. 1980
Error Analysis of the Spoken English of College Students in Gurdaspur District. Thesis (Ph. D.) — Punjabi University, Patiala.

882. BHATIA, Aban Tavadia. 1974
"An Error Analysis of Students' Composition." *IRAL*. 22 : 4. pp. 337-350.

883. DHAR, K.L. 1966
"Spelling Errors in English of Elementary School Teachers." *The Progress of Education.* Jan. pp. 225-227

884. —.1967
Report on the Errors in the Written English of Graduate Teachers of Himachal Pradesh. Solan, Himachal English Language Teaching Centre.

885. —. 1967
Report on the Errors in the Written English of Matriculate Teachers of Himachal Pradesh. Solan, Himachal Pradesh English Language Teaching Centre.

886. —. 1967
Some Interesting Frequencies of Common Errors in the English of Trained Matriculate and Trained Graduate Teachers. Solan, Himachal Pradesh, English Language Teaching Centre.

887. D'SOUZA, Jean. 1976
An Error Analysis and Its Pedagogical Implications : A Study within the Conceptual Framework of Traditional

Competence Composition Written by Goan Students. Thesis (M. Litt.)—Central Institute of English and Foreign Languages, Hyderabad.

888. ELISHA, C.S. 1967
The Influence of Telugu on the English Spelling of Telugus. Manchester, Manchester University.

889. GROVER, P. 1972
"Misuse of Indian English." *Hindustan Times.* 9. Jun.

890. INDAPURKAR, C.D. 1968
A Linguistic Study of Errors in English of the Middle School Pupils of Chandrapur (Chand) District of North East Maharashtra. Thesis (Ph.D.)—University of Poona, Poona.

891. —. 1973
"Spelling Errors in English : A Descriptive Study." *Journal of the Gujarat Research Society.* pp. 12-25.

892. JACKSON, Howard. 1979
"Errors of Punjabi Learners of English : A Comparison of the Grammars of Punjabi and English." *CORE.* 3/3.

893. JAIN, Mahavir. 1069
Error Analysis af an Indian English Corpus. Edinburgh, Unniversity of Edinburgh. (Unpublished papers.)

894. —.
Errors Analysis of an Indian English Corpus, *IN* RICHARDS, Jack C. (ed) : *Error Analysis.* London Longman. (Also in : BHATNAGAR, Y.C. (ed) : *Readings in Foreign Language Teaching in India.* New Delhi, Ajanta, 1983. pp. 194-224.)

895. JOSHI, Mahendra Iswarlal.
Error Analysis and Remedial Teaching in English with Reference to the First-Year College Learners of English in South Gujarat. Thesis (Ph. D.) —South Gujarat University.

896. MARTHA, Mary. 1974
Remedial Drills—Khasi Speakers' Spoken English. Thesis

(M. Litt.)—Central Institute of English and Foreign Languages, Hyderabad.

897. MARWEIN, Martha Mary. 1977
Error Analysis of the Khasi Students Written English at the College Entry Level. Thesis (M. Litt.)—Central Institute of English and Foreign Languages, Hyderabad.

898. MEHROTRA, Raja Ram. 1971
"Correctness in the Use of English : A Teacher's Dilemma." *The Education Quarterly*. 23 : 3. pp. 41-42.

899. NEELAKANTAN, Susheela. 1978
Errors at the Discourse Level : A Study of Errors in English (at the Discourse Level) Made by First-Year English Medium Students (in the Twin Cities of Hyderabad and Secunderabad). Thesis (M. Litt.)—Central Institute of English and Foreign Language. Hyderabad:

900. PARASHER, S.V. 1974
An Analysis of Errors in the English Pronuciation of a Group of Hindi-Speaking M.A. (English) Students in Madhya Pradesh. Hyderabad Central Institute of English and Foreign Languages. (Diploma Paper.)

901. ———. 1977
Errors in English Made by a Group of Hindi Speaking First Year Students of Madhya Pradesh. Thesis (M. Litt.) Central Institute of English and Foreign Languages, Hyderabad.

902. PARIDA, D.S. 1985
Error Analysis of Written English of Class VIII Student of Orissa. Thesis. (Ph.D.)—Ravishankar University, Raipur.

903. PARTHASARATHY, G. 1968
Remedial Lessons on English Pronunciation for Use in the Language Laboratory. Thesis (Research Diploma) —Central Institute of English and Foreign Languages, Hyderabad.

904. PASSE, H.A. 1955
The Use and Abuse of English : Common Errors in Ceylon English. Madras, Oxford University Press.

905. PATRIKAR, Moreshwar Sadashivrao.
Linguistic Analysis af the Error in *Written English of the Students of B.A. Class of the College* in *Urban Centres of Vidarbha.* Thesis (Ph. D.) —Nagpur University, Nagpur.

906. PEARSE—SMITH, T.L.N. 1934
English Errors in Indian Schools. Bombay.

907. RAMPTON, M.B.H. 1983
"Some Flaws in Educational Discussion of the English of Asian School Children in Britain." *Journal of Multilingual and Multicultural Development.* 4 : 1. pp.15-28.

908. SAGAR, B.M. 1984
" Abuse of English in Our Colleges." *Journal of Indian Education.* 10 : 3. pp. 35-42.

909. SAH, Prajapati Prasad. 1966
A Comparative and Descriptive Analysis of Errors by the Hindi Speaking Students of English. London, University of London. (Unpublished paper.)

910. ——. 1971
"Towards a Theory of Error Analysis." *York Papers in Linguistics.* 1. pp. 29-65.

911. SAHGAL, Anju and AGNIHOTRI, Rama Kant. 1986
"Dictation as a Diagnostic Test." Indian *Journal of Applied Linguistics.* 12 ; 1-2. pp. 119-126.

912. SESHADRI, C.V. 1966-67
Error Analysis. Annamalainagar, Annamalai University (Diploma paper.) (This work studies the common errors made by the students in Their English writing.)

913. SHARMA, S.K. 1974
Linguistics Study of Errors in the Written English of Students Joining B.A. in the Hindi Speaking Area. Thesis (Ph. D.) Meerut University.

914. SMITH-PEARSE, T.L.N. 1934
English Errors in Indian Schools Bombay, Oxford University, Press.

915. SOGANI, R. 1977
General English at the Undergraduate Levels : Effectiveness and Relevance : A Study of the English Teaching-Learning Situation in Delhi University. Thesis (M. Litt.) Central Institute of English and Foreign Languages, Hyderabad.

916. SREEVANI, Sistla. 1985
An Analysis of the Errors Made in Use of Indirect Speech by Telugu Learners of English at the Secondary *Level.* Thesis (M. Litt.)—Central Institute of English and Foreign Languages, Hyderabad.

917. SRIVASTAVA, Indra Swarup. 1966
"An Analysis of Common Errors in Intermediate English." *Teaching English* (Bombay). 9 : 1. pp. 26-38.

918. ——. 1963
"Remedial Teaching of English Pronunciation." *Teaching English.* 8 : 1. pp. 18-22.

919. ——. 1964
"Linguistic Difficulties of Hindi Pupils Learning English a Second Language." *Teaching English.* 8 : 2. pp. 37.-

920. SRIVASTAVA, Shanti Svarup. 1970
Hindi Maatr Bhaasaa Angrezii Siikhane Me Hone Vaalii Trutiyo Kaa Adhyayan. (A Study of Errors Made in Learning English for Hindi Mother—Tongue Speakers.) Thesis (Ph. D.)—K.M. Institute, Agra.

921. TAYLOR, Harvey M. and KIRSHANA RAO, A.V. 1981.

"Indian English 'Errors' and American English Usage." *IRAL.* 19 : 2. pp. 137-147.

922. TIWARI, Ashok. 1985
"Spelling Errors Arising From Incorrect Pronunciation." *Journal of Indian Education.* 11 : 4. pp. 36-40.

923. TONGUE, R.K. 1975
"Problems of Remedial English Teaching at Secondary and College Level." *Newsletter, Central Institute of English and Foreign Languages.* 11. pp. 13-16.

924. VERMA, Shivendra Kishore. 1962
A Study of Errors in English Made by Hindi-Speaking Students in Bihar. Edinburgh, School of Applied Linguistics, University of Edinburgh. (Unpublished paper).

925. ———. 1969
"Contrastive Studies and Error Analysis." *Rajasthan Board Journal of Education.* 5 : 4. pp. 3-13

926. VORA, I.A. 1966
A Study of Syntactical Mistakes in English. Vallabh Vidyanagar.

927. WHITWORTH, George C. 1907
Indian English : An Examination of Errors of Idiom Made by Indians in Writing English. Letchworth, Herts, Garden City Press. (Later edition published in 1932 from Lahore).

928. WILBER-FORCE, Bell H. 1917
"Corruptions of English in the Indian Vernacularies." *Indian Antiquary.* 46.

10. STYLISTICS

929. ALAM, Qaiser Zoha. 1979
"*Kanthapura's* Style : A Point of View." *Language Forum.* 5 : 2. pp. 27-37.

930. ———. 1980
"*Train to Pakistan*—A Model of New Journalism." *Language Forum*. 4 : 1-2. pp. 47-57.

931. AMUR, G.S. 1978
Manohar Malgonkar and the Problem of the Indian Novelist in English, *IN* MOHAN, Ramesh. (ed) : *Indian Writing in English*. Bombay, Orient Longman. pp. 37-46.

932. ANNIAH GOWDA, H.H. 1976
"The English of the Indians and the Africans in Their Fiction." *The Literary Half-Yearly*. 17 : 1. pp. 23-38.

933. ATMARAM. 1984
The Linguistic Devices in Indian English of Raja Rao and Mulk Raj Anand, *IN* ATMARAM : *Essays on the Indian English Literature*. Khadekeshwar, Aurangabad, Parimal. pp. 8-25.

934. BADVE, V.V. 1974
Experimentation with Language With Reference to Manohar Malgonkar's Novels, *IN* DESAI, S.K. (ed) : *Experimentation With Language in Indian Writing in English (Fiction)*. Kolhapur, Shivaji University.

935. BELLIAPPA, N. Meena. 1967
East-West Encounter : Indian Women Writers of Fiction in English, *IN* NARASIMHAIAH, C.D. (ed) : *Fiction and the Reading Public in India*. Mysore, University of Mysore. pp. 18-27.

936. CHASWAL, Balram. 1973
The Stylistic Development of Mulk Raj Anand. Thesis (Research Diploma)—Central Institute of English and Foreign Languages, Hyderabad.

937. DAS, Bikram K. 1971
"A Stylistic Analysis of the Speech of the Indian Characters in Forster's *A Passage to India*." *The Indian Journal of English Studies*. 12. pp. 42-54.

938. DATTA, J. 1960.
"Indo-English Creative Writers." *Quest*. Winter.

939. DESAI, Shantinath K. (ed). 1974
Experimentation With Language in Indian Writing in English (Fiction). Kolhapur, Department of English, Shivaji University.

940. DESAI, Shantinath K. 1974
Transplantation of English : Raja Rao's Experimentation With English in His Works of Fiction, IN DESAI, Shantinath K. (ed) : *Experimentation With Language in Indian Writing in English (Fiction)*. Kolhapur, Department of English, Shivaji University.

941. DISSANAYAKE, Wimal. 1985
"Towards a Decolonised English : South Asian Creativity in Fiction." *World Englishes*. 4 : 2. pp. 233-242.

942. DORION, Mark. 1984
"To Convey in a Language That is Not One's Own the Spirit That is One's Own : Understanding Non-Native English Speakers Through an Awareness of Their Native Culture and Literature." *The Journal of the Indian Writing in English*. 14 : 1. pp. 33-48.

943. DUBEY, Vinod Shankar. 1982
Style of English Newspapers in India : A Linguistic Study. Thesis (Ph. D.)—Bhagalpur University, Bhagalpur.

944. ———. 1978
A Stylistic Analysis of Mulk Raj Anand's Seven Summers : A Dialectal Perspective. Thesis (M.A.)—Department of Linguistics, University College of North Wales. (Unpublished.)

945. ENG, Oor Boo. 1974
"Indian Poets and the Use of English." *Journal of Commonwealth Literature*. 9. pp. 10-20.

946. GALANTE, Lovetta Lynn. 1984
"Nativization and Characterization in Raja Rao's *Kanthapura*. Amos Tutuola's *The Palm-Wine Drinkard* and Chinua Achebe's *A Man of the People*." *The Journal of Indian Writing in English*. 14 : 1. pp. 20.31.

947. GOKAK, Vinayak Krishna. 1978
The Concept of Indianness with Reference to Indian Writing in English, *IN* MOHAN, Ramesh. (ed) : *Indian Writing in English*. Bombay, Orient Longman. pp. 21-25.

948. GOUD, L.M. 1974
Indianisms in the Works of R.K. Narayan, *IN* DESAI, S.K. (ed) : *Experimentation with Language in Indian Writing in English* (*Fiction*). Kolhapur, Shivaji University.

949. GURU PRASAD, Thakur. 1974
Experimentation With Language in Indo-Anglian Fiction:A Note Towards Definition of Traits in the Works of Mulk Raj Anand, *IN* DESAI, S.K. (ed) : *Experimentation with Language in Indian Writing in English* (*Fiction*) Kolhapur, Shivaji University.

950. JOSEPH, Margaret P. 1978
"In Defence of Indian Writing in English." *Freedom First*. No. 313. Dec. pp, 6-7.

951. JUSSAWALA, Feroza. 1983
Family Quarrels : Towards a Criticism of Indian Writing in English. Thesis (Ph. D.)—University of Utah.

952. KACHRU, Braj B. 1984
"The Bilingual's Creativity : Discoursal and Stylistic Strategies in Contact Literatures in English," *Studies in the Linguistic Sciences*. 13 : 2. pp. 37-55. (Also in : *Language Forum*. 10 : 1-4. 1984-85. pp. 21-46.)

953. ———. 1964
"A Note on Indian Writing in English. (Comments)" *Harvard Educational Review*. Winter.

954. ———. 1970
Some Style Features of South Asian English, *IN* GOODWIN, K.L. (ed) : *National Identity*. London, Heinemann Educational Books. pp. 122-137.

955. KALIA, K.A. 1972
Mulk Raj Anand's Linguistic Devices (in *Untouchable*). Hyderabad, Central Institute of English and Foreign Languages, Hyderabad. (Diploma paper).

956. KAUL, R.K. 1973
"The Problem of Speech in Indo-Anglian Writing." *Quest*. No. 85. pp. 65-68.

957. KULSHRESTHA, Chirantan. 1982
Half-Baked Thoughts on the Unhoused Muse, *IN* NARASIMHAIAH, C.D. and SRINATH, C.N. (eds) ; *English : Its Complementary Role in India*. Mysore, Dhvanyaloka. pp. 67-74.

958. LABRU, G.L. 1968
Indian Newspaper English. Thesis (Diploma)—University of Leeds.

959. ———. 1984
Indian Newspaper English. Delhi, B.R. Publishing.

960. LAL, P. 1964
"Indian Writing in English." *Harvard Educational Review*. 34 ; 2. pp. 316-319.

961. ———. 1967
"English and English Writing in India." *Conspectus*. 2 : 2. pp. 37-47.

962. ———. 1969
Modern Indian Poetry in English. Calcutta, Writers Workshop.

963. ———1974
Gandhiji's English, *IN* LAL, P. : *The Lemon Tree of Modern Sex. Literary Essays*. Calcutta, Writers Workshop. pp. 42-46.

964. LUTHRA, Alka. 1982
"Indo-English Writing : More Kiplinesque Than Indian." *Surya India*. 6 : 6. Mar. pp. 56-57.

965. MASSON, S.P. 1974
A Stylistic Analysis of Kamala Markandaya's Novel *The Coffer Dams*. Hyderabad, Central Institute of English and Foreign Languages. (Unpublished paper.)

966. MCCUTCHION, David, 1969
Indian Writing in English : Critical Essays. Calcutta, Writers Workshop. Chapters 2 and 4.

967. MENON, Usha. 1975
The Indianness of Indian English : An Examination of Features Specifically Indian in Indo-Anglian Fiction. Calicut.

968. MISAL, Nanda
Indian English Prose Style : Some Explorations. Thesis (M. Phil.)—Shivaji University, Kolhapur.

969. MOHAN, Ramesh. 1978
Some Aspects of Style and Language in Indian English Fiction, *IN* MOHAN, Ramesh. (ed) : *Indian Writing in English*. Madras, Orient Longman. pp. 192-202.

970. MOHAMMED, U. 1971
Some Stylistic Features of Menon S. Martha's *The Sale of an Island*. Hyderabad, Central Institute of English and Foreign Languages. (Unpublished Diploma paper.)

971. MOKASHI-PUNEKAR, Shankar. 1972
The Indo-Anglian Creed and Other Essays. Calcutta, Writers Workshop. pp. 28-72.

972. ————. 1978
Indian Writing in English: A Statement of Some Stylistic Issues, *IN* MOHAN, Ramesh (ed) : *Indian Writing in English*. Madras, Orient Longman. pp. 140-149.

973. MOKTALI, Laxmi R. 1974
Experiments With Language in Kamala Markandaya's Novels : *Nectar in a Sieve* and *Some Inner Fury*, *IN* DESAI, S.K. (ed) : *Experimentation With Language in Indian Writing in English* (*Fiction*). Kolhapur, Shivaji University.

974. MUKHERJEE, Meenakshi. 1978
The Language of the Indo-Anglian Novelist, *IN* MOHAN, Ramesh. (ed) : *Indian Writing in English*. Madras, Orient Longman. pp. 150-156.

975. ————. 1970
"Style in Indo-Anglian Fiction." *Indian Writing Today*. 4 : 1. pp. 6-13.

976. NAIK, M.K. 1982
"Achievement of Indian English Fiction." *Journal of the Karnataka University* (*Social Sciences*). 26. pp. 1-9.

977. NAMBIAR, K.C. 1976
Stylistic Studies in Indian Writing in English—A Suggested Framework, *IN* MOHAN, Ramesh. (ed) : *Indian Writing in English*. Madras, Orient Longman. pp. 157-172.

978. NAND, V.G. 1970
A Stylistic and Structural Analysis of the Last Chapter of R.K. Narayan's *The Guide*. Hyderabad, Central Institute of English and Foreign Languages. (Unpublished Diploma paper.)

979. NARANG, G.L.
English Deictic Reference Items as Cohesive Devices in Some of R.K. Narayan's Novels. Thesis (Ph.D.)—Kurukshetra University, Kurukshetra. (In progress.)

980. NARASIMHAIAH, Closepet Dasappa. 1970
National Identity in Literature and Language : Its Range and Depth in the Novels of Raja Rao, *IN* *National Identity : Papers Delivered at the Common-*

wealth Literature Conference, University of Queensland, Brisbane, 1967. pp. 153-168.

981. NARASIMHAN, Raji. 1975
"Indo-English : Criticism Without Criteria." *Indian Horizon.* 34 : 1. pp. 49- .

982. ————. 1979
"Indo-English ; The Inclusive Voice." *Indian Literature.* 22 : 6. pp. 32-41.

983. ————. 1981
"Indo-English : New Depths, New Dimensions." *Indian Literature.* 24 : 6. pp. 24-33.

984. PANDEY, G.S. 1970
A Linguistic Approach to 'The Continent of Circe' by Nirad C. Chaudhuri. Hyderabad, Central Institute of English and Foreign Languages. (Diploma paper.)

985 PANIGRAHI, P.K. 1982
A Stylistic Analysis of the Poems of Jayanta Mahapatra. Thesis (M.Litt.)—Central Institute of English and Foreign Languages, Hyderabad.

986 PATHAK, R.S. 1986
"The Nativization of English in India and O.P. Bhatnagar's Exploitation of Lexical Resources." *Language Forum.* 12. pp. 99-123.

987. PATHAK, S.N. 1973
Unusual Collocations and Compounds in 'Coolie' by Mulk Raj Anand. Hyderabad, Central Institute of English and Foreign Languages. (Diploma paper.)

988. PATIL, Chandrashekar. 1969
The Kannada Element in Raja Rao's Prose : With Reference to 'Kanthapura'. Hyderabad, Central Institute of English and Foreign Languages. (Unpublished Diploma paper.)

989. PATNAIK, B.N. 1984-85
"Stylistics and the ELT Programme in India." *Language Forum.* 10 : 1-4. pp. 147-160

990. PETERS, John D. 1984
"Some American Reflection on Indian Writing in English." *The Journal of Indian Writing in English* 14 : 1. pp. 1-9.

991. PRAKASH, Ravendra. 1973
A Stylistic Study of Raja Rao's 'The Serpent and the Rope'. Thesis (Research Diploma)—Central Institute of English and Foreign Languages, Hyderabad.

992. PRASAD, Baidya Nath. 1979
The Language of Raja Rao's *The Serpent and the Rope*, *IN* SINHA, Krishna Nandan. (ed) : *Indian Writing in English*. New Delhi, Heritage. pp. 29-41.

993. RAJAN, Balachandra. 1965
"The Indian Virtue." *Journal of Commonwealth Literature*. 1. Sep. pp. 80-81.

994. RAJENDRAN, A.V. 1982
A Stylistic Analysis of the Poetry of Kamala Das. Thesis (M.Litt.)—Central Institute of English and Foreign Languages, Hyderabad.

995. RAJNATH. 1977
"Indo-Anglian Literature : A Critical Muddle." *Statesman*. 1 Jan.

996. RAMAKRISHNAN, R. 1971
Stylistic Studies in Indo-Anglian Poetry. Thesis (Research Diploma)—Central Institute of English and Foreign Languages, Hyderabad.

997. RUSSELL, A. 1986
"A Linguistic Assessment of Indo-English Poetry of Our Time." *Language Forum*. 12 : 1-2. (Forthcoming.)

998. SARANG, Vilas Govind. 1978
English and Marathi : Stylistic Aspects of Literary Translation. Thesis (Ph.D.)—Indiana University.

999. SHAHANE, Vasant A. 1982
"Some Aspects of the Indian English Writer's Creative Use of English." *Literary Criterion.* 17 : 1. pp. 75-88.

1000. SHARMA, Nar Deo. 1986
"Stylistics of Indian English Poets." *Language Forum.* 12 : 1-2. (Forthcoming.)

1001. SHARMA, J.P. 1980
Linguistic Modifications (English for Indian Sensibility), *IN* SHARMA, J.P. : *Raja Rao : A Visionary Indo-Anglian Fiction.* Meerut, Shalabh Book House. pp. 94-115.

1002. SINGH, V.D. 1975
"Indian English and Indo-Anglian Poetry." Paper presented at the All India English Teachers' Conference, Madurai.

1003. SIVADASAN, C.P. 1972
A Stylistic Comparison of Three Editorials of The Times (London) and The Hindu (Madras). Hyderabad, Central Institute of English and Foreign Languages. (Unpublished Diploma paper.)

1004. ————. 1977
Linguistic Experimentation in Contemporary Indian Verse in English. Thesis (Ph.D,)—Calicut University.

1005. SRIDHAR, S.N. 1982
Non-Native Literatures : Context and Relevance. *IN* KACHRU, Braj B. (ed) : *The Other Tongue : English Across Cultures.* Urbana, University of Illinois Press. pp. 291-306.

1006. ————. 1982
Westernization of Indian Literary Forms, *IN* KACHRU, Braj B. (ed) : *The Other Tongue : English Across Cultures.* Urbana, University of Illinois Press.

1007. SUBRAHMANIAN, K. 1977
"Penchant for the Florid. (With Comments by C.H. Prator, P. Strevens, J.D. Brown and K. Srinivasa Iyengar)" *English Language Forum.* 15. pp. 23-24. (Also in : *CIEFL Newsletter.* 13 : 4. 1977. pp. 18-25 and *Indian Writing in English,* edited by Ramesh Mohan. Madras, Orient Longman, 1978.)

1008. VARMA, Ravi S. 1981
"Hindustani Words in Mulk Raj Anand." Paper presented at XI All India Conference of Dravidian Linguists, 5-7 Jun. 1981, Department of Linguistics, Osmania University, Hyderabad. (Abstract published in *Souvenir.* pp. 62-63.) (Also in : *Language Forum.* 12 : 1-2. 1986.)

1009. VAYANGANKAR, B.V. 1974
"Khushwant Singh's Experimentation With Language With Reference to *Train to Pakistan*", *IN* DESAI, S.K. (ed) : *Experimentation With Language in Indian Writing in English* (*Fiction*). Kolhapur, Shivaji University.

1010. VENKATESWARAN, Shyamala. 1970
"The Language of Kamala Markandaya's Novels." *The Literary Criterion.* 9 : 3. pp. 57-67.

1011. VERGHESE, Cherukothu Paul. 1971
Problems of the Indian Creative Writer in English. Bombay, Somaiya.

1012. VISVESWARAIAH, H.S. 1972
A Stylistic Analysis of Representative Passages of Raja Rao's 'The Serpent and the Rope'. Hyderabad, Central Institute of English and Foreign Languages. (Unpublished Diploma paper.)

1013. WALI, S.K. 1974
A Stylistic Study of 'Nectar in a Sieve' by Kamala Markandaya. Thesis (Research Diploma)—Central Institute of English and Foreign Languages, Hyderabad.

1014. WEIR, Ann Lowry. 1982.
Style Range in New English Literatures, *IN* KACHRU, Braj B. (ed) : *The Other Tongue* : *English Across Cultures*. Urbana, Illinois, The University of Illinois Press. pp. 307-322.

1015. WENDT, Allan. 1978
Babu to Sahib : Contemporary Indian Literature, *IN* MANUEL, M. and AYYAPPA PANIKER, K. (eds): *English and India*. Madras, Macmillan. pp. 94-107.

AUTHOR INDEX

SUBJECT INDEX